A Practical Guide to Archaeological Photography

D0160832

Carol L. Howell
Warren Blanc

Archaeological Research Tools 6
The Institute of Archaeology
University of California, Los Angeles
1992

LIBRARY
ST. LOUIS COMMUNITY COLLEGE
AT FLORISSANT VALLEY

UCLA Institute of Archaeology Editorial Board

Jeanne E. Arnold, Marilyn P. Beaudry-Corbett,

Timothy K. Earle, Ernestine S. Elster,

Richard Janko, Richard M. Leventhal,

Sarah P. Morris, and James R. Sackett

UCLA Institute of Archaeology

Richard M. Leventhal, Director

Ernestine S. Elster, Director of Publications

Photographs by Carol L. Howell

Edited by Brenda Johnson-Grau,

with help from Beverly Godwin, Pat Campbell Healy,

Marilyn Gatto, Ellen Hardy, and Judith Rasson

Designed by Brenda Johnson-Grau

Production by Tim Seymour, Wendy Lau, Dan Villalpando,

and Angela Cohen

Library of Congress Cataloging-in-Publication Data

Howell, Carol L.

A practical guide to archaeological photography / by Carol L.

Howell and Warren Blanc.

p.   cm. — (Archaeological research tools ; 6)

Includes bibliographical references (p.) and index.

ISBN 0-917956-73-7

1. Photography in archaeology. I. Blanc, Warren. II. University
of California, Los Angeles. Institute of Archaeology. III. Title.
IV. Series: Archaeological research tools ; v. 6.

CC79.P46H68 1992

778.9'9301—dc20   92-46804

                                    CIP

Copyright © 1992. Regents of the University of California.

All rights reserved. Printed in the USA.

Contents

Preface

When packing for my first archaeological expedition, I was careful to weigh the advantages of taking extra socks over more granola bars, but I did take plenty of film. I have never since undertaken anything that has proven to be as rewarding, nor do I think that I ever worked as hard. (If I recall correctly, I ended up short on socks, long on granola bars, and out of film.)

With more than twenty-five years of experience with a 35mm camera, I find that the task of documenting fieldwork can be overwhelming. Just as an anthropologist draws upon various disciplines, so, too, does the archaeological photographer—using techniques practiced by photographers specializing in landscape, studio, architecture, travel, and photojournalism and applying them in archaeological contexts.

Both the site and the fieldwork must be documented for the project record, and any diagnostic elements of related artifacts must be recorded for future analysis—on archive-quality film. Photographs for presentations or publication are also necessary. All this must be accomplished in a remote field situation with no more equipment than the photographer can carry.

So why would anyone do this more than once? Because you forget the aggravation and the discomfort. I enjoy testing my techniques against the rigors of fieldwork. From discussions with professional, avocational, and student researchers in the field, I have developed a keen appreciation for the perceptions of the trained eye. I have also become disconcerted by the inability of many researchers to turn their unique perception into photographic data. Exposure to classroom and seminar presentations, attendance at professional meetings, and consultation with many archaeological researchers have further reinforced my conviction that most archaeologists are not master photographers, most do not want to master photography, and most need not master photography. With access to some basic information on what the camera can—and cannot—do, along with suggestions on techniques that work well in given field situations, most archaeologists can, however, take very good pictures.

My friend and collaborator Warren Blanc patiently listened to me recount my perception of the need and agreed to aid in the development of this solution: a practical guide to archaeological photography. He comes from a family of photographers, and his low-key approach and realistic ideas all reflect the thinking of a person who is as comfortable behind the lens as he is under the hood of his MG. In his chapter (7), he gives practical suggestions for those who wish to acquire basic studio equipment and leads the reader through some simple steps to getting professional results.

The thoughtful comments and advice offered by photographers Bill Tate and James Grady have also added to this text, and the eagerness of many archaeology students to learn and to share their skills has been encouraging. My favorite flintnapper and illustrator, Keith Abernathy, gave me the benefit of his expertise and his patience. Archaeologists David Browman, Katharina Schreiber, Jane Stone, and Mark Sutton offered a perspective for which I am grateful. The kind people at the UCLA Institute of Archaeology extended their nurturing attitude through Ernestine S. Elster. Jonathan Kent not only suggested the need for such a text but also encouraged the process— prodding, poking, reviewing, commenting, editing, and, in general, helping it happen.

I hope that this problem-solving approach will aid you in attaining research goals. Archaeological data are terrible things to waste.

— Carol L. Howell

Introduction

Good photographs are an integral part of good archaeology. The researcher of today must have the photographic skills to document the research process; record data accurately; produce publication-quality photographs; convey information to others; and assemble and maintain an archive-quality resource. Assuming the responsibility of recording an archaeological project is therefore a considerable commitment. Furthermore, you can count on only one opportunity to photograph fieldwork because you can't recreate an excavation and you can't assume that you will be returning to a remote location or that a site will remain intact for later reconnaissance. And when the site is in a foreign country, all the artifacts may have to stay behind. This guide will help prepare you to meet these objectives with increased confidence and success—regardless of your current level of photographic expertise.

FOCUSING ON 35MM

Most books on archaeological photography favor *large-format cameras* for fieldwork. Large-format cameras can produce images that are $2^1/_4$ inches square, four-by-five inches, or larger. The longest side of a 35mm slide is thirty-five millimeters in length (about $1^1/_2$ inches). Large-format cameras can create beautiful large prints like the ones in museum catalogs or posters. The outstanding quality of 35mm lenses and films has, however, made the large-format cameras obsolete for fieldwork. (The 35mm slide is also standard for classroom or seminar presentations.) Today's 35mm cameras are technological marvels. Manufacturing advances in the last ten years have combined better quality lenses with simplified operation, at prices that most people—even archaeologists—can afford. And it's easier to fit a large amount of equipment into a small camera bag.

Some novice photographers think that using an automatic 35mm camera involves simply pointing the camera at the subject, pressing the shutter, and that's it. This point-and-shoot method will work much of the time. Producing an accurate record of archaeological research may require more and therefore compels us to avoid common mistakes and to learn to take advantage of some of the camera's unique attributes.

Replacing Your Camera Manual: Have you misplaced the booklet that describes the workings of your camera? Try writing to the manufacturer for information or check with your local library.

YOUR CAMERA

The explanations and examples presented in this guide assume that you use a simple no-frills manual 35mm camera, which means that you will understand some of its mechanics, or a completely automatic system, which does everything except pay for itself. There are two general categories of 35mm cameras:

Single lens reflex (SLR): In this system, the image coming through the lens is bounced off a mirror to the eye of the photographer. This system supports more creative photography because when the lens is changed or accessories are added, you can immediately see exactly how the image has changed.

Rangefinder: In this system, the photographer looks through a viewing window parallel to the lens rather than through the lens. There are few accessories available because the photographer cannot change the view in the window to match any change to the lens. And, at very short distances, the viewing window is not aimed at the same place as the lens. Rangefinder cameras are smaller, lighter, and less expensive than SLR cameras.

If your camera is an automatic, the choice of settings may be limited, but you can learn to use those options appropriately. The booklet that came with the camera will indicate whether any of the following is possible:

- A completely manual system allows you to set both shutter speed and f-stop.

- A shutter priority system lets you select the shutter speed; the camera sets the appropriate f-stop.

- An aperture priority system lets you select the f-stop; the camera sets the shutter speed.

- Means of overriding the meter to intentionally over- or underexpose a scene.

If there is no way to adjust any of the settings, this guide will still help you learn why attention must be given to careful handling of the camera when taking a photograph—especially in dim light; why you will produce a more detailed photograph by getting the camera into the best position for a particular subject; why film does not "see" light the same way that you do; why you should test your camera to determine exactly how close to a subject you can focus; and why some pictures are just plain difficult to take. You will learn to compensate for poor light conditions or for a subject with awkward dimensions.

Even with an automatic camera, you can influence results. If your camera gives you a choice between automatic settings or manual adjustments, take the time to become familiar with each of these modes. You might practice by taking the same picture in both automatic and manual mode until you spend more time thinking about the subject than the camera. It is not as easy to use the manual settings, but using them gives you valuable, creative options.

Those who have previous experience with manual 35mm cameras may rate your experience as minimal or extensive. This guide addresses many levels of expertise and hopes to aid the novice without boring the proficient. If you feel comfortable with your knowledge of the camera, you needn't wade through lessons designed for a beginner. Read "Lens Basics" in chapter 1 and "Film Latitude" and "Metering Pitfalls" in chapter 2 and decide whether you need to review those chapters completely before continuing. If you are experienced in wildlife or sports photography, review the checklist in appendix A. You may find some of the tricks for achieving maximum resolution and taking close-ups helpful.

CAMERA AS TOOL

During training, an archaeologist gains a basic knowledge of mapping, learns to turn observation into a comprehensive set of field notes, and becomes adept at selecting from a variety of tools. All these skills are adapted to given field conditions and are refined with experience. This same approach is useful to photography: with a basic understanding of the camera as a multifaceted tool, you can adapt your knowledge to any number of situations.

Like a beginning illustrator, the beginning photographer does not start by getting every possible accessory. The artist must first learn the differences among pencils, then how to choose the proper one for a particular task. In photography, you begin by learning the mechanics of shutter speeds and f-stops. These distinguish a 35mm camera from a snapshot camera. When you can make an informed choice among these variables, you will have graduated from taking snapshots to taking photographs and you are ready to adapt this tool to fieldwork.

PREPARING FOR FIELDWORK

Time spent in the field is fleeting. When it is over you may have only fond memories, reports, as many illustrations as could be completed in the field, and photographs. The degree of a project's success is often enhanced by, if not dependent on, photographs that provide enough data for unequivocal interpretation.

In addition to helping you gain a productive familiarity with the camera, this book addresses equipment maintenance. Ordinarily, you may take only two or three rolls of film in a year. In the field, you'll be taking a dozen or more—depleting battery life. You'll also be working in conditions that can easily impair mechanical function.

The type of film that you use and how you handle it is another consideration—given that it will determine whether your photographs will be worth looking at ten, fifty, or a hundred years from now. Some photographic documentation of archaeological research (as well as dissertation and postdoctoral research) is worthless because of an ill-considered choice of film or a destructive method of handling. Because they are historical documents, old photographs make an ongoing contribution to archaeology. To ensure the survival of your photographs, you must consider a good deal more than the sale price when choosing film.

Handling film with care is not difficult and does not require an elaborate routine. In the field, take precautions to protect it from heat, moisture, and dirt. When film is returned from the processor, make sure to label slides, prints, and negatives with field notes. Later, we'll explore practical ways to balance the demands of archival storage with the need for accessible data.

IN THE FIELD

We'll give examples of common situations in the field. Many of the problem-solving suggestions are in response to worst-case conditions—that is, situations in which routine point-and-shoot photography usually fails. It is assumed you will be traveling to a remote location for an extended period; working with the amount of equipment that you can carry; coping with conditions that may include wind, heat, not enough light, or light that produces too much contrast; and not returning to the site to retake pictures that did not turn out.

A minimal amount of equipment is recommended, given the problems of transportation, as well as expense, in the field. Good photographs seldom require specialized accessories. More often, they are the result of recognizing potential problems and taking the time to use proven techniques.

Other books may advise a more complex approach to photo reconnaissance, but the methods suggested in this guide are practical and in keeping with what you can expect to accomplish on a small project in a remote location with limited access to resources. I would never, for example, send my camera into the prevailing winds attached to a helium-filled balloon, and therefore I do not propose it as an alternative. If you wish to send someone else's camera up in a balloon, see Harp (1975). Similarly, chartering a plane to do your own aerial mapping is not practical for most archaeological projects. However, should you get lucky enough to hitch a ride in a small plane, I include some hints that will help you make the most of the opportunity.

IN THE STUDIO

In the section on taking photos in the studio, you'll come in out of the elements and learn to work with accessories that plug in and turn on. (Few field laboratories will have the range of accessories employed in the studio.) Some of this simple equipment will help you photograph many artifacts. The importance of good technique is discussed, and some insight into achieving professional results is offered.

A STEP-BY-STEP APPROACH

Novice photographers often spend much time poring over the "how to load film in the camera" section of their manual. Though it soon becomes routine, this task can at first be nerve-racking. In this guide, you'll learn some of the more sophisticated camera techniques incrementally. We'll begin by teaching you the basics:

Selecting the proper shutter speed

Working with the meter to vary the exposure

Choosing the best f-stop for the subject

Changing lenses when necessary

As your knowledge increases, your skill will be evident: your photographs will be consistently well-exposed and detailed. Once using good technique is second nature to you, make a point of coming back to these pages. Explore the depth-of-field guide and consider some of the close-up accessories or filters that may be useful for your project. Start carrying a tripod. Reacquaint yourself with your camera's manual and, if possible, master the art of taking a double exposure. It can be informative—as well as exciting—to view both sides of an artifact in a single picture.

The first few chapters are devoted to the basics of using a 35mm camera. Examples illustrate how various camera features can be used. In the index, you'll find these collated under the heading "Techniques." Use these examples to refresh your memory and to supplement chapter 6, which gives examples of field situations.

At the end of the book in a chapter called "Review," you'll find a collection of points to consider. Taking the time to look at this chapter again before a field season should help you maintain good technique. This chapter is also designed so that you can cut out individual sections, paste them onto index cards, and place the cards in your camera bag or notebook.

As you face the challenges of photographing fieldwork, learn from your successes and failures. You will have the chance to make your own mistakes. Make the most of them by using this text to figure out what went wrong (see also the troubleshooting guide in appendix A).

From an unaesthetic profile of a grid to an exciting sequence of an artifact as it is excavated, good camera technique will make sure that your project is well documented. In addition to making you a better archaeologist, your increased sophistication in using the camera will make picture taking more creative and pleasurable.

Chapter One

Understanding Camera Function

When introduced in 1925, the 35mm camera got the attention of photographers because, unlike large-format cameras, it could be carried up a mountainside easily or used unnoticed in a crowd. Its size was not, however, its most appealing feature. After all, Eastman had been marketing small snapshot cameras since 1888. With a 35mm camera, however, the phototographer retains control of focusing the lens and adjusting the exposure. A high-quality lens that can be focused sharply on any subject has clear advantages over a lens that has been factory set to focus at twelve feet to infinity. Why anyone would deliberately choose to fool around with exposure settings is not so obvious.

Let's start by taking some of the mystery out of these settings. The *shutter speed* is the length of time that the camera shutter is open—that is, the length of time that the film is exposed to light. The *aperture* is an opening inside the lens, which can be reduced or enlarged to control the amount of light passing through the lens to the film.

The relationship between these two settings can be compared to the irrigation of a field. To irrigate a field, a farmer must have *x* amount of water. To allow the necessary amount of water into the field, the irrigation gate can be opened halfway for four hours or all the way for two hours. Erosion and evaporation aside, the result is the same. Similarly, if a good exposure requires *x* amount of light to reach the film, you can open the camera's aperture to allow lots of light and use a fast shutter speed. Or, you can narrow the aperture to let in less light and use a longer shutter speed.

If the result is the same, why would anyone choose to fool around with exposure settings? Because each setting can have an effect—subtle or dramatic—on the resulting photograph. Fast shutter speeds can freeze action, capturing a bird in flight or the splash of a diver. Lengthy shutter speeds are necessary in dim light—for a nighttime view of a city, the interior of a cave, or an archaeological site before dawn or near sunset.

In the field, you seldom have the luxury of waiting for better conditions; so, different shutter speeds are useful. For example, two miles from camp at sunset on the last day of a site survey, you use a lengthy shutter speed to take the picture or do without.

Using a Tripod: Tripods are especially useful for archaeological photography because post-fieldwork analysis is often aided by the details gathered when using a minimum-size aperture.

Why then don't we simply use one size aperture and control light with just the shutter speed? Because the size of the aperture determines how much of the picture will be in focus. Before lenses were developed for cameras, pinhole cameras were all that were available. Pinhole-sized apertures can capture amazingly detailed images, but a good exposure takes a very long time to get. Enlarging the aperture causes the image to become fuzzy. Lenses were developed to keep the subject in focus.

With a large aperture and a fast shutter speed, we can get a nice photograph of Aunt Betty, though not much else in the picture will be very sharp. With a small aperture and a slow shutter speed, we can capture a picture of Aunt Betty standing beside her sports car at the tennis court—with everything from the hood ornament to the linesman in detail. With a small (pinhole) aperture, you can lie in the dirt alongside a grid and get a good photograph of the profile of the far wall, as well as every detail in the foreground excavation. Using a large aperture would leave some of the details fuzzy. Depending on where the camera is focused, either the floor of the excavation or the far profile is sharp. The rest of the information is lost in a blur.

Why don't we use small apertures and slow shutter speeds all the time? Because when the light is dim, you may need an exposure as long as one-half second, and the camera will have to be mounted securely on a tripod to ensure a steady exposure. Without a tripod, you can use only faster, hand-held shutter speeds with a larger aperture.

LENS BASICS

Camera lenses fall into these general categories:

Standard lenses take in a 45° angle of view (about what the eye sees).

Wide-angle lenses take in a broader angle of view, usually 60° to 80°. Compared with a normal lens, a wide angle lets you gather more information. Everything must, however, be reduced to fit it all in.

Telephoto lenses enlarge a slice of the normal view (like a pair of binoculars), 12° to 30° depending on the length of your lens.

The size of a lens is stated in terms of its *focal length,* which is the distance from the optical center of the lens to the film. Look at the front of a lens to read its size:

- Standard lenses range from 49mm to 52mm.

- Wide-angle lenses are snub nosed and commonly run from 28mm to 35mm. A 28mm takes in a wider angle than a 35mm, though both are good field lenses.

- Telephoto lenses are long and usually run from 80mm to 200mm. The 135mm is popular and easy to pack. A 200mm lens is more powerful; it takes one-sixteenth of the view through a standard lens and enlarges it to fill the picture, but it is also larger and heavier than a 135mm.

- Zoom lenses can shift a single lens from one focal length to another, for example, from 28mm to 50mm or anywhere in between. More convenient, these can be a practical alternative to using two or three lenses with set focal lengths.

This range of lenses, from 28mm to 200mm, is useful in the field. Lenses that take in a wider angle (8mm to 24mm) usually cause so much distortion to a subject that they are impractical for documenting a site. Longer telephoto lenses (from 300mm to 400mm) are so big that they must be supported by their own tripod and are impractical on a cross-country site survey.

There is no one perfect lens for fieldwork. With a wide-angle lens, you can stand alongside a two-meter excavation grid and get the whole thing in the photograph. You could, however, take overlapping photographs to get from corner to corner with a standard lens. With telephoto lenses, you can sometimes photograph the inaccessible. Like a pair of binoculars, a telephoto lens can capture a site across a raging river or on the other side of the valley. If you have only the standard 50mm lens, your first step should be to pit the demands of your project against what you can accomplish with your lens. Eventually, however, you will probably want a lens in each of the groups (normal, wide, and telephoto). Before you buy, see appendix B.

SHUTTER SPEEDS

A standard 50mm lens can encompass a 45° angle of view. A 200mm lens reduces this angle to about 12°. A small amount of camera shake, creating a movement of only .5°, affects these two lenses differently. In addition to exaggerating the slightest movement, the longer lenses can cause awkward weight distribution, which only compounds the problem. Therefore, pay attention to the focal length of the lens on the camera when selecting an appropriate hand-held shutter speed. The rule of thumb used by professionals is that the focal length of a lens dictates the slowest hand-held shutter speed (table 1.1). If you need to shoot at slower speeds, get out a tripod. This rule may seem conservative, but it can help you start getting consistently sharp results.

Diagnosing Problems with Shutter Speed

Your camera can take pictures, hand-held, at a 60th of a second or faster. You can probably hold your breath and shoot at a 30th, and on a good day maybe even a 15th. However, many people unknowingly fail to get consistently sharp pictures *even at a 60th.* Diagnosing problems related to shutter speed can be difficult. For example,

- The photograph is not obviously blurred—but it does not have that overall sharpness that some others do.

- The subject is not in focus—but a closer look reveals that nothing is in focus.

- The weather was hazy, you say—but the sky is dark blue.

- The photograph is good enough to keep—but you have to explain it to each viewer because the details are not clear.

- The photograph is not sharp and you conclude that the filter was of poor quality—but the replacement filter gives the same results.

If any of these examples are familiar, *heed speed.* Ill-chosen shutter speeds may be impairing your ability to record and convey accurately the details of your research.

Table 1.1 Lens focal length and minimum shutter speed.

Lens focal length	Minimum shutter speed
28 mm to 70 mm	60th of a second
80 mm to 135 mm	125th of a second
180 mm to 200 mm	250th of a second

Testing the Steadiness of Your Hand: To test your steadiness with a camera, set the focus of your standard lens at its minimum—about eight inches. Walk up to a well-lit fence or wall until you have a clear view of a knot, the edge of a brick, or some other linear detail. Take the same picture at a 15th, 30th, 60th, and 125th in the same manner you normally do. This test will give you a good idea of how much information you can gain when the shutter speed is fast enough. If the subject were a finely incised vessel or a piece of fabric with an interesting weave, the extra sharpness could be important to later analysis.

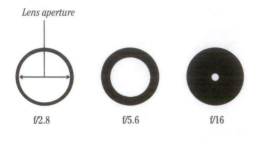

Lens aperture

f/2.8   f/5.6   f/16

Figure 1.1 Aperture sizes.

Table 1.2 Speed and f-stop sequences.

Speed (in seconds)	f-stop
<<	<<
$1/_{500}$	f/2
$1/_{250}$	f/2.8
$1/_{125}$	f/4
$1/_{60}$	f/5.6
$1/_{30}$	f/8
$1/_{15}$	f/11
$1/_{8}$	f/16
$1/_{4}$	f/22
>>	>>

Table 1.3 Reciprocal settings.

Larger aperture, faster speed

Metered exposure	60th at f/5.6
	30th at f/8
	15th at f/11
	8th at f/16
	4th at f/22

Smaller aperture, slower speed

Note: All these combinations produce the same exposure.

APERTURES AND F-STOPS

The aperture of the camera is the lens opening through which the light passes. The relative *size* of the aperture is noted on the lens in increments called *f-stops* (fig. 1.1). Selecting an appropriate f-stop is important. Understanding the correlation between the lens's aperture and a selected f-stop will help you to choose confidently and accurately.

As the f-stop number increases, the size of the aperture decreases. Remember this inverse relationship. With practice, observing it will become second nature. Until then, it may help to recall that the f-stop numbers run in a sequence opposite to what common sense might dictate:

Small f-stop numbers (2, 2.8)   large aperture (lots of light through the lens)

Large f-stop numbers (16, 22)   small aperture (minimal light through the lens)

On occasion, you may deliberately increase or decrease the amount of light in an exposure to make the subject a little lighter or darker. If the subject is going to be too dark, you can add light by moving to a lower f-stop (from f/5.6 to f/4). If the subject seems too brightly lit, you can reduce light by moving to a higher f-stop (from f/5.6 to f/8, for example).

Shutter Speeds and f-stops

The camera's shutter speed determines the length of time that the shutter will be open to allow light to pass through to the film. The camera's f-stop determines how much light is gathered in this given length of time. Both have an ordered series of settings (table 1.2). Each increment serves to double or halve the function of the adjacent setting:

Speed   From 250th to 500th, the shutter is open half as long. The length of the exposure is reduced by half. From 250th to 125th, the exposure is doubled.

f-stop   From f/4 to 2.8 (one full stop), the amount of light that will pass through the lens is doubled. From f/4 to f/5.6, half as much light is gathered.

Table 1.3 illustrates the reciprocal nature of shutter speeds and f-stops.

Using Reciprocity

Now that you understand how reciprocity works, you could easily handle the following situation:

1. With a hand-held camera and a 135mm telephoto lens, you take a meter reading of a 30th of a second at f/16.
2. This speed is too slow, however, to record the details of the subject reliably, and so...
3. You move the speed dial two settings faster to 125th and open the aperture two full stops to f/8, which permits you to shoot with the assurance that all the details will be captured.

If you are uncertain as to why the adjustments were made, take a moment to review.

DEPTH OF FIELD

Pinhole cameras, which capture light to pass through a pinhole-sized aperture, produce very detailed images; however, this type of camera can take hours to gather enough light for a good exposure. Nowadays, cameras use a larger aperture along with a lens to keep a particular area in focus. The term *depth of field* is used to describe the area in focus; that is,

Field	Area or zone around the subject. If the camera is focused until only the subject presents a detailed image, an area around the subject is also going to be in sharp focus: the field of sharpness.
Depth	Size of this field of sharpness.

For example, we may have a very sharp image only at a distance of six to seven feet—a depth of field of one foot. For a portrait, a photographer might deliberately use this narrow depth of field to blur unimportant details behind the subject. Other parts of the scene will not distract the viewer. For a landscape, a photographer may want to have every detail in sharp focus, from the fence in the foreground to the mountains on the horizon. The camera is then adjusted for a maximum depth of field, which may run from seven feet to infinity.

Any newspaper offers examples of how depth of field is used. Photographs of sporting events isolate the athletes in brilliant detail while the crowd is just a blur—using a narrow depth of field. Photographs of real estate capture all the details of foreground and background—using a large depth of field.

In a site photograph, the depth of field must be gauged appropriately or important details can inadvertently be reduced to an indecipherable blur.

Point of Focus

When you focus a camera on a subject, the *point* at which you focus—as well as an area in front of and behind this point—will be sharp in the final photograph. This entire area, near to far, is the depth of field. Do not rely simply on the view through the lens to determine exactly what the depth of field will take in—how much of the picture is actually going to be in focus. You need to understand how the depth of field relates to the point of focus and then how to influence its size.

Point of focus	The one sharp image you see in the viewfinder—arrived at by turning the camera's focusing ring.
Depth of field	The area, both in front and behind the point of focus, that will be sharp in the final photograph.

Figures 1.2 and 1.3 demonstrate the function and limitations of depth of field and suggest specific application for using this valuable tool. In the first instance, the point of focus is between the edge and the neck of the jar. The depth of field extends in front of, and behind, the point of focus to make the visible portion of the subject sharp (fig. 1.2). The point at which the camera is focused is one-third of the way into the depth of field—that is, the depth of field extends one-third in front and two-thirds behind the point of focus.

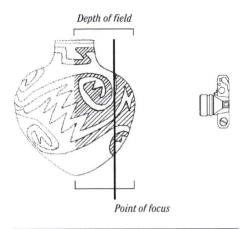

Figure 1.2 Focus behind front edge of vessel.

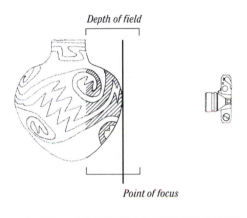

Figure 1.3 Focus on front edge, wasting depth.

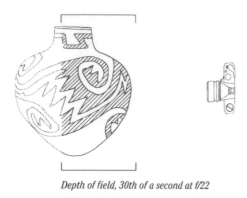

Depth of field, 30th of a second at f/22

Figure 1.4 Maximum depth, high f-stop.

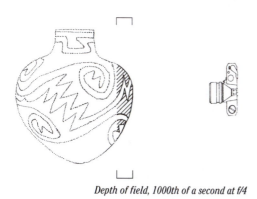

Depth of field, 1000th of a second at f/4

Figure 1.5 Minimum depth, low f-stop.

Table 1.4 Depth variation by distance and f-stop with standard 50mm lens.

Distance (to subject)	Depth at f/4	Depth at f/16
10 feet	3 feet	18 feet
3 feet	2 inches	10 inches
2 feet	1 inch	4 inches
15 inches	$\frac{1}{2}$ inch	2 inches

Without knowing this, I might have focused on the front edge of the jar, wasting foreground sharpness and blurring the neck and sides of the vessel (fig. 1.3).

Changing the Size of the Depth of Field

The *size* of the depth of field (that is, the distance of near-to-far sharpness) is determined by a combination of the selected f-stop (aperture size) and the distance of camera to subject. By being alert to these variables, we can learn to spot circumstances when it may be helpful to adjust camera settings or placement.

The higher the f-stop, the greater the depth of field. In figures 1.4 and 1.5, the 50mm lens is focused at a distance of two feet. With an exposure of a 30th of a second at f/22 (fig. 1.4), depth of field is about six inches. With an exposure of a 1000th of a second at f/4 (fig 1.5), depth of field is about one inch. Both of these combinations of speed and f-stop will give the same exposure. A high f-stop (f/22) gives a depth of field of about six inches: the subject is very detailed overall. A low f-stop (f/4) reduces the depth of field to about one inch: most of the subject is out of focus. A narrow depth of field may be desirable or, with careful positioning of the camera, at least acceptable.

The closer the subject, the narrower the depth of field. The fifteen-inch to three-foot distances noted in table 1.4 are often used in fieldwork for features or artifacts. Depth of field is reduced when using a low f-stop (such as f/4). In close-up photography, this effect is dramatically compounded (see figure 1.6).

At a "safe" f/16, note the difference in depth of field when the subject is at 3 feet and at 2 feet (see the right column of table 1.4). It is all too easy, even at f/16, to run out of depth before we run out of subject. Don't add to your problems by using a type of film that requires slow shutter speeds, a low f-stop, or both, by hand-holding the camera (the slightest movement is exaggerated with a close-up), or by working in less than bright sunlight. (A few clouds, a subject in shadow, or a museum interior could limit you to f/4.)

Using a different type of film, putting the camera on a tripod, or adding a flash are all ways to get back to a higher f-stop. We'll be looking at each of these later. For right now, let's examine a few techniques for dealing with the worst-case conditions outlined above. By recognizing that we could be in trouble with such a paucity of depth, we have already made progress.

Working with the Plane of the Film

Keep in mind that the camera and its depth of field have a single *plane* and the subject has one or more revealing *planes*. A document, a textile fragment, or a small assortment of lithics can easily require focusing as close as 18 inches. With a flat subject, a depth of field of one inch or less may be more than adequate. The camera must be positioned so that this small depth of field is placed evenly across the surface of the subject. As shown on the left of figure 1.7, the photographer simply walked up and took the picture; 90 percent of the layout will be out of focus, and no one will notice the 10 percent that is sharp. On the right, the camera is *centered* over the layout.

a

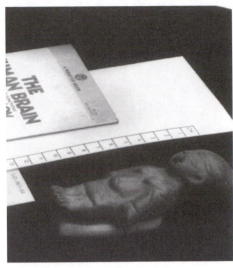

d

b

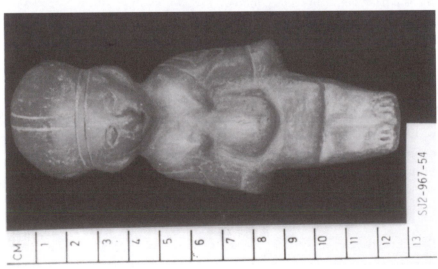

c

Figure 1.6 This Ecuadorian figurine has been set up in two different ways. On a white background, with a ruler, this picture (a) was taken, with a hand-held camera, at a 60th of a second, f/5.6. With only a fraction of an inch for depth of field, the focus is on the mouth. In the next picture (b), with minimum depth of field, only the face is in sharp focus. In the final picture (c), depth of field extends from the nose to the hands, and the scale is sharp and easy to read. View (d) shows the setup of the final picture: the figurine is placed on a black velvet background. Putty was used to lift the body of the figurine into the same plane as the face. The book alongside the figurine holds the scale and catalog number within the same sharp plane. Using a tripod and an exposure of 1/4 second at f/22, I focus on the ear of the figurine.

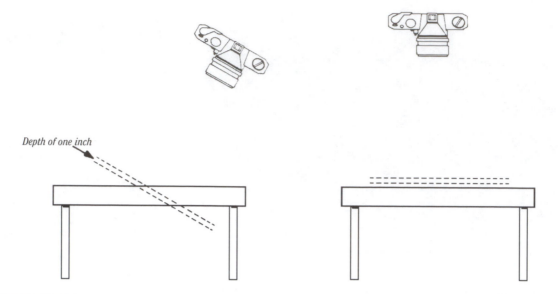

Figure 1.7 Matching the plane of the camera to the plane of the subject.

The photographer matched the film plane (the back of the camera) to the subject. (To work at this angle, you may have to stand on a chair or set the subject on the floor.)

When the subject is not as conveniently flat, a half an inch of sharpness can't capture every detail. By recognizing its most important plane, however, you can still get a good picture. The vessel in figure 1.8, for example, has several points to be considered. First, you can turn the camera 90° to use the rectangular format, as it best suits the subject.

Because the vessel is small enough to require that the camera be set at its minimum focus, after setting the camera, focus on the subject by moving the camera back and forth, rather than by turning the focusing ring. (Holding the camera steady and focusing by moving the camera lets you maintain a comfortable grip, ready to squeeze the shutter at the right moment.)

The meager depth of field will capture the best information if it is placed along plane *a* (as noted in figure 1.8). The camera is positioned at this angle by moving it until both the upper and lower parts of the vessel that touch plane *a* have come into sharp focus.

Finally, push the camera very slightly, moving the point of focus into the subject (to plane *b*), and take the picture—taking advantage of that little bit of sharpness between the point of focus and the camera. To focus in this manner, away from the center of the picture, you must use a Fresnel focusing screen (see chapter 4). With this type of focusing screen, when the image is out of focus, it is broken up into hundreds of blurred specks. A split-image, on the other hand, comes together as you focus, allowing you to focus only at the center of the picture. In this example, because you need to focus in two places simultaneously, such a focusing screen would not work. Fortunately, some cameras come with a combination of these two focusing-screen designs, and some have interchangeable styles.

Focal Length

When the distance from the subject is unchangeable, being able to use a different type of lens is an advantage. In a museum, for example, a moderate telephoto lens (80mm to 135mm) can capture a large image of a small artifact in the back of a display case. By changing to a telephoto, though, I not only magnified the image but also created a problem with depth of field.

With a light meter reading, we can determine the f-stop and shutter speed settings for a good exposure with any lens. The size of the aperture at f/8 on a 50mm lens is, however, smaller than an f/8 aperture on a 135mm lens. Even though the size of the aperture is different and the shutter speed remains the same, the exposure is the same because light is lost as it travels through a long telephoto lens. The amount of light that reaches the film is the same in both instances; we allow for this loss with a long lens, and so the size of the aperture is larger: *the larger the aperture, the smaller the depth of field.*

The size of the aperture on a wide-angle lens, set at this same f/8, is therefore smaller still, given that the shorter wide-angle lens loses less light than the standard 50mm lens. At f/8, the wide-angle lens produces a larger depth of field than the 50mm. The 50mm lens produces a larger depth of field than the 135mm.

Any time you change to a lens with a longer focal length, you sacrifice depth of field. This principle holds true for zoom lenses as well. When you zoom from 50mm to 135mm, the size of the depth of field is reduced.

Recognizing potential problems is half the battle. Choice of f-stops and lenses and the distance to the subject will all influence how much of the picture is going to be in focus. In the next section we'll learn to predetermine the depth of field.

Predetermining Depth of Field

Determining how much of a picture is going to be in focus is our next topic. First we'll learn to use a guide that is right there on the camera. It is a simple and very useful tool with many applications to fieldwork. You can astonish your friends and impress your colleagues when you focus the camera without looking through the viewfinder.

As an aid to focusing, lenses are designed to stay at their largest aperture (providing maximum viewing light) until the shutter is pressed. When the shutter is released, the aperture closes to the chosen f-stop as the picture is taken. Many cameras, however, have a previewing system that allows us to close the aperture to the selected f-stop before taking the picture to assess the depth of field visually. When the f-stop is above f/8 or when light is dim, unfortunately, the amount of light that we see through the lens is reduced to the point that a visual assessment is usually unreliable.

Practice with your camera set at its minimum focus to learn how close you can get to your subject and how much depth of field you can count on at various f-stops. For example, your project might need some photographs documenting small artifacts or extremely small things, such as the cut marks on a bone or the number of wefts to a warp. Using table 1.5, you can determine whether the picture you are about to take is going to have a depth of field of three inches or three-sixteenths of an inch, a distinction that can be critical. To use this generic depth-of-field guide,

Look at the subject with the camera to determine the amount of magnification.

Apply this specification to the chart.

Read the depth of field for any given f-stop.

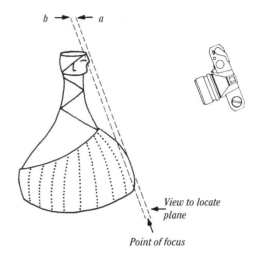

Figure 1.8 Plane of three-dimensional subject and point of focus.

View to locate plane

Point of focus

Table 1.5 Magnification and depth of field (in inches).

Narrow axis	Magnification (of subject)	f/2	f/4	f/8	f/16	f/22
10	.1X	1/2	1	2	4 1/4	6
6.5	.15X	1/4	1/2	1	2	2 3/4
5	.2X	5/32	1/4	9/16	1 1/8	1 5/8
4	.25X	3/32	3/16	3/8	3/4	1
3	.3X	1/16	1/8	1/4	1/2	3/4*
2	.5X	1/32	1/16	1/8	1/4*	3/8*
1	1X	**	1/64	1/32	1/16*	3/32*
.5	2X	**	**	1/64*	1/32*	1/16*

* Not recommended because of poor resolution.

** See Bibliography for references on close-ups.

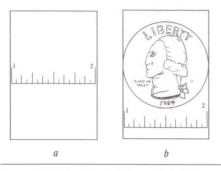

Figure 1.9 (a) One-inch rule (1X magniifcation); (b) US quarter (1X magnification).

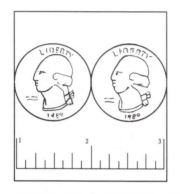

Figure 1.10 Two quarters and two-inch rule (.5X magnification).

Figure 1.11 Mug and four-inch rule (.25X magnification).

Figure 1.12 Plate and ten-inch rule (.1X magnification).

By relating these data to magnification, you can use this technique with any set-focal-length lens. Let's look at how to arrive at magnification. The image recorded on a 35mm slide or negative film measures one by one and a half inch. If you could focus extremely close to a ruler so that you see only one inch along the narrower axis of the frame, you would have a 1X (life size) magnification (fig. 1.9a). (Some macro lenses can do this; others may need extension tubes or plus lenses; see chapter 4.) A US quarter is close enough to an inch in diameter so that if it fills the frame, the magnification is 1X (fig. 1.9b). If the quarter extends to just the center of the frame (or if the ruler reads two inches), the magnification is .5X (fig. 1.10). Without the benefit of any close-up attachments, many lenses can focus on an area as small as four inches. The image of our Anasazi mug is one-fourth actual size, a magnification of .25X (fig. 1.11). Finally, if we want to shoot a fair-sized ceramic plate, the distance across this axis could be ten inches, or a magnification of .1X (fig. 1.12).

When you are ready to take the picture, use a ruler at the point of focus to measure the narrow axis of the frame (just as we did with the plate). Table 1.5 uses this measurement (left column) to determine the depth of field for the f-stop. If the narrow axis of your view takes in four inches, for example, and the camera is set at f/16, the depth of field is three-quarters of an inch. To make the most of this little bit of sharpness, remember that because the depth of field extends one-third in front of the point of focus and two-thirds behind it, the depth of field extends one-fourth inch in front of that one sharp image that you see through the lens and one-half inch behind it. If three-quarters of an inch doesn't cover the subject, you may be able to use a higher f-stop (f/22 or f/32). Combined with a slower shutter speed, the higher f-stop will give a larger depth of field.

You could also take this picture using the depth where it gives you the most information on detail. Then back up a little bit. By reducing the image size to a five-inch field of view, you can get a depth of field of one and an eighth inches. It may seem a tiny amount, but a little goes a long way with a small artifact.

The figures in table 1.5 are for most standard lenses with a set focal length of 35mm to 105mm. The table also allows for the use of extension tubes. If you use a longer telephoto, wide-angle, or zoom lens, or add magnifying diopters, the depth of field will be decreased slightly.

Use caution when you move in close to get a great big image of a small subject. If it doesn't work, use a tripod and this table and place the depth of field where it will do the most good.

If your project needs a two-quarter–sized picture, you may need to shop for a close-up (macro) lens or accessory that will give you a good .5X magnification. (See chapter 4.) If you can now get as close as .25X and come up with an attachment that doubles magnification, you're home free. Do not hesitate to take your camera and a couple of quarters along when you shop.

Depth-of-Field Guide

At least 90 percent of all manual lenses have a built-in depth-of-field guide. Few recreational photographers have any cause to use it, but archaeologists do. If you have a manual-focus camera, it will be helpful at this point to get it out. (The guide on the camera may vary slightly from the illustration in figure 1.13a.) The depth-of-field guide is made up of *pairs* of numbers that represent the upper range of f-stops. (These numbers may not all be included on your lens, or they may simply be color coded to the f-stop numbers.) Each number has a line leading to the distance scale. Depth of field is read *from* the distance scale *in between* these pairs of f-numbers. In figure 1.13a, the lens is focused at a distance of four and a half feet. The aperture is set at f/22. I look at the pair of 22 indicators on the depth-of-field guide. Relating these to the distance scale, I see that my depth of field will range from about three and a half feet to seven feet. If the f-stop is moved to f/16, the distance between the 16s is read, which means the area in focus will be from about three and seven-tenths to six feet (fig. 1.13b).

In figure 1.13c, I focus at infinity and use f/22. Depth of field extends from about twelve feet to infinity. There is an interesting foreground feature at a distance of seven feet that I want to include in the shot, and so I move the infinity mark to the left, keeping it within the 22s (fig. 1.13d). The area of sharpness is increased to a range of six and a half feet to infinity.

The built-in depth-of-field guide has many uses. On a visit to a mound site, for example, I had enough light to hand-hold the camera at f/16. Moving the infinity mark back to the 16 on the depth-of-field guide, I knew that the area from ten feet to infinity was in focus. The scene was a grass-covered expanse of an ancient plaza with a central mound—nothing very dramatic. Estimating a point ten feet in front of me, I bent to include this in the picture. This minor adjustment added environmental information, perspective, and a bit of interest as the foreground invites the viewer into the scene.

EXERCISES

The following examples illustrate the basic camera techniques covered so far. In most of these, we look at ways to meet some clearly established objectives. It is easy to go through much film in a field season, but quantity does not ensure a complete record. When you prepare to take a picture, pause to consider objectives. Are you overwhelmed with nondescript candid photographs? Photos that receive no better than half a smile on the first shuffle through the stack? Taking the effort to produce very sharp photographs is essential to good photography, but it will never make up for poor composition. Break yourself of the bad habit of hurriedly pointing and shooting. As you prepare to depress the shutter, take a moment to look at everything in the frame. For example,

- Is that a bright orange bucket off to the side? Does it add information or does it distract from the subject?

- Is that a big footprint in your otherwise well-manicured grid? Take the time to sweep it out—it will be noticed.

- Is the horizon level? Does the edge of the grid run parallel to the edge of the photograph? Odd angles can be disorienting.

- Can you find a better angle? How about moving in the pickup truck to where you can stand on it. Perhaps lying in the dirt for a ground-level view will help.

- Could you get closer?

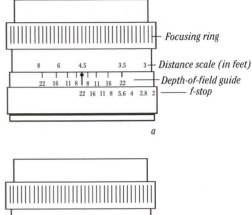

a

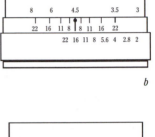

b

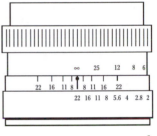

c

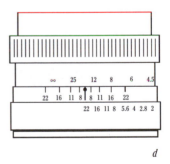

d

Figure 1.13 (a) Lens with labeled depth-of-field guide, f/22; (b) depth at f/16; (c) depth at infinity; and (d) infinity moved to f/22. (Metric measurements on distance scale are not illustrated.)

- If you turned the camera 90°, would you get a better picture?

- Is the background the same color as the subject? Is it hard to tell where the subject stops and the background begins? Would walking around the subject for a different angle of light help? Can you get an assistant to reflect a little more light on the subject so that it stands out from the background?

- Is there a tree (seemingly) growing out of the subject?

- Are you close enough to the laborers so that this scene is a clear demonstration of fieldwork?

- Is it another guess-who-was-bent-over-in-the-unit shot?

- Finally, why are you taking this picture?

Go for the Subject

Get close to your subject. Then get closer. The amateur photograph is most readily identified by the amount of wasted space surrounding the subject. The space is unimportant and the subject is underrepresented. Overcome timidity, dispense with good manners, and go for the subject. "Fill the frame" means fill that picture with a large, detailed image.

Wildlife photographers (aka dwellers in duck blinds) know that their subject must cover 30 to 50 percent of the frame, 50 percent of the overall picture. Without a large image, they will not be able to tell a *Pipilo fuscus* from a *Sturnus vulgaris*. If you hope to have an image large enough to identify a particular feature, design element, or technology, keep this 50-percent rule in mind.

The Comprehensive View

Be it urban neighborhood or the entire mountain valley, a comprehensive view should be one of your first objectives (fig. 1.14). If there is better light later on and you have the chance to take another picture, do it. Don't make the common mistake of putting this picture off until the last day of the field season, when you may have to shoot in the rain or at 6 PM when the others are in the car ready to leave. Such a panorama shot is important because it contributes necessary environmental information to the project record; future researchers who may be trying to follow up on your work will be better able to pinpoint the location; and it will help to establish context when you present the results of your work to others. (See chapters 3 and 5 for some tips on using a black-and-white contact print to collect comprehensive site information.)

An overall photograph of a site gives valuable information on relationships of features within a site and on its surroundings (fig. 1.15a) and contributes to the sense of context. Everything in this scene must be in sharp focus, from the background vegetation to the evidence of use on the floor in the foreground. This area of habitation must be fully represented. Such pictures often have a fuzzy foreground—a result of simply focusing at infinity and taking the picture. It not only obscures information but also distracts the viewer, who must work to discern important elements. Your reputation as

a

b

c

Figure 1.14 The Lord of Sipan was smiling when I visited Huaca Rajada. Overcast skies allowed me to capture many details. In this part of the ongoing excavation, archaeologists have left an intrusive burial in situ. Changing from a wide-angle to a telephoto lens produces an informative sequence (a, b, c)

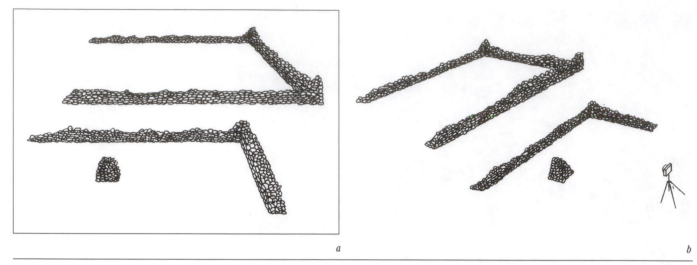

a   b

Figure 1.15 (a) "Photo" of entire site; (b) possible placement of camera.

a researcher who records data accurately will suffer because such data presentation is sloppy.

In figure 1.15b, a camera set up with a 50mm lens can get it all in focus. However, the foreground wall would be crowding the frame. The viewer may wonder where it goes (and what is left out). Because the objective is to view the site as a whole, I may try to back up a nearby incline or bring in a pickup truck to stand on. A revealing perspective could thereby be obtained and all features kept well within the picture. Or I could change to a wide-angle lens, which would bring enough of the foreground into the picture for the viewer to comprehend that the entire room is represented.

Reducing Depth of Field for Emphasis

To show how the pillar relates to the room (fig. 1.16a), the depth of field must be reduced to cover only this room—because the wall of the adjacent room (in the background) is irrelevant and distracting. To make the interior wall stand out from the background, the far wall must be so far out of focus that it is not viewed as part of the picture. To achieve this emphasis, determine how much depth of field you need. The distance that needs to be covered is from the closest point in the foreground to the interior wall (fig. 1.16b).

The depth of field must extend only from six to fifteen feet. Relating these parameters *from* the distance scale *to* the depth-of-field guide, I discover that I can limit the area of sharpness to six to fifteen feet by using f/8 (fig. 1.17). (The illustration uses a wide-angle lens.) In our first example of using the depth-of-field guide, we read the depth for a given f-stop. In this case, set distances are applied to the depth-of-field guide, and the guide then tells us which f-stop to use.

The aperture is set at f/8, then the meter must be checked to find the appropriate shutter speed. The focus is set by the depth-of-field guide; resist the urge to refocus. It is important that the six- and fifteen-foot distances stay within the pair of 8s on the depth-of-field guide while the picture is being taken.

If my distance estimator is dysfunctional, I find an object on the front edge of the foreground, focus on it, and read the distance from the camera lens. The same process may be followed for determining the distance to the interior wall.

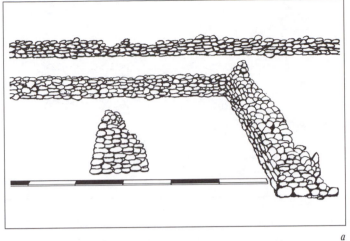

a

b

Using Image Magnification for Capturing Detail

In the next picture, I need to capture comparative information. The material and technology used to construct the pillar is different from that of the wall. I would like to show this variation in a single photograph (fig. 1.18); the details of both pillar and wall must, therefore, be sharp. Measuring the distances to the foreground and to the wall, I find that my 50 mm lens will just barely provide the depth I require (three and a half to seven feet using f/22). Changing to a wide-angle lens to get more depth would also give more wall and much less wall detail.

Gaining *comparative* detail means getting the most magnification possible with the 50 mm lens. Without the most magnification, there's no reason to take the picture. After double-checking distances, I make certain that three and a half feet and seven feet are between the 22 lines on the depth-of-field guide, which places the point of focus at just over four and a half feet, or somewhere behind the pillar. This scene is going to look incredibly bad through the lens: neither pillar nor wall will be in focus. Overcome the temptation to refocus the camera; the depth-of-field guide really does work.

Using Reciprocal Settings for Lengthy Exposures

It is late in the day and I have fussed around with f-stops while the sun has been setting. After all the deliberation that went into selecting f/22 for this last scene, I now find that I don't have enough light. The meter says I must open the aperture to f/11 and use this with my slowest shutter speed, one second. What good is f/11 when I need f/22? Knowing that speeds and f-stops are reciprocal and that each setting is double (or half of) the next, I move the f-stop two settings from f/11 to f/22. I then double the one-second shutter speed *twice*:

f/11	1 second
f/16	2 seconds
f/22	4 seconds

To get a four-second exposure, we must set the speed dial on a B, or timed, setting. This holds the shutter open as long as the shutter button is depressed. Using a cable release to press the shutter, I hold it open while

Figure 1.16 (a) "Photo" of room and pillar; (b) room, camera, and depth to be covered.

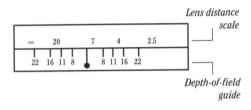

Figure 1.17 Distance scale and depth-of-field guide.

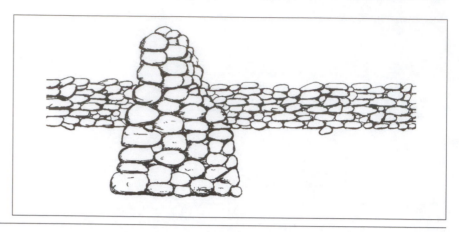

Figure 1.18 "Photo" of pillar and wall.

counting the necessary four seconds. This practice may seem like more than you care to deal with, but it is one I resort to frequently when using a very small aperture.

The light does not have to be especially dim. An overcast sky can also cause this type of problem. This technique is also useful indoors, in a cave, a basement, or a kiva. When you need all the depth of field your highest f-stop provides, and the meter gives you a one-second exposure at too low an f-stop, *double* the exposure for every increase in f-stop. Because we have taken extra pains to get this picture, let's take a couple more to be sure that it turns out. In this situation, I would try four-, six-, and eight-second exposures. One will be just right.

Failure of reciprocity: When using this technique with any exposure over one second, you can run into a problem called "failure of reciprocity." The light sensitivity of a film is rated on a brief exposure to bright light. Most outdoor films are not recommended for exposures of more than one second: the light is so weak that uneven penetration of the various color-sensitive layers of the film occurs. Often you can overcome this characteristic failure by doubling even this lengthy exposure.

Stratigraphic Profiles and Depth of Field

It is not often that our vantage point allows us to center the camera on a unit wall, eliminating the rest of the excavation from view. Usually the scene must include a portion of the floor and adjacent walls in the foreground. Because you cannot assume that these attendant features are unimportant, you must make sure that the depth of field covers the entire area. For a good perspective of the wall, I may try lying in the dirt on the opposite side of the unit. Through the lens, my view may, for example, take in a three- to six-foot distance. I find these distances on the camera's distance scale; center them on the depth-of-field guide and learn that, if I use f/16, both three and six feet will be in focus; and set the camera for f/16 and take a meter reading to determine the shutter speed.

If the shutter speed is slower than a 60th of a second, use a tripod to hold the camera steady—because even the slightest camera movement will blur the image and waste the depth-of-field advantage.

Before taking the picture, look through the camera to make sure the horizon is level and everything in the view is neat. When you do this, do *not* adjust the focus so that the wall looks sharp—the focus has already been determined by setting three feet and six feet between the pair of 16s on the depth-of-field guide.

Chapter Two

Working with Light

Now that we have considered the technical aspects of producing a sharp photograph, we need to consider how to achieve a good exposure consistently. What could be worse than having to discard the photo record of the research process because of careless over- or underexposure? What *could* be worse might be recording an orange-on-cream slip diagnostic sherd as a rust-brown-on-tan slip. Bad data can be worse than no data.

"Good light" is what photographers dream of, pray for, and make sacrifices to the gods in the hope of getting. "Good light" is whatever light is best for your subject, and it is fleeting. When you see it, use it:

Bright sunlight gives you the opportunity to climb a hillside and record your site when its features are most distinct. Many sites are constructed, literally, from the earth that they stand on. Without the added definition of a highlight along the top of a wall or a shadow that outlines a window and sets off the length of a foundation, a site can visually melt into the ground.

Lightly overcast weather (as well as the minutes just before sunrise or just after sunset) is very good for photographing the features of a grid or profile. There will be enough directional light for depth and definition, but neither highlight nor shadow is so extreme that details will be obscured.

Heavy overcast weather (or uniform shade) is great for photographing artifacts. No dark shadows will hide a finely incised design element. No bright reflections will bounce off a polished surface or fade the numbers on a scale.

Enough daydreaming about the blessings of good light. Conditions are seldom so cooperative in the field. Light can be troublesome. In fact, light is almost always troublesome. Expect too much or too little. Fleeting clouds will put splotches across a site and force you to change your exposure every three seconds. It's not amusing either, because it usually happens at the midpoint in the excavation, the site has been cleaned, the crew is standing around, and you must get this picture.

Note: Chapter 6 gives examples of ways to cope with poor light, including using a reflector or a strobe to add light or using a shade to reduce contrast.

MEASURING LIGHT

First, we need to understand the mechanics of measuring and recording light. The human eye handles light very efficiently. On a sunny street or in a dark alley, the eye adjusts instantly to changing levels of light. The eye's adaptive ability means that we seldom need to think about brightness or darkness. The eye can adjust to a very broad *latitude*.

As photographers, we need to remind ourselves that as we look at a scene, our eye is continually adjusting for light and dark areas. When we look at the bright parts of a scene, we see everything that is there. Slightly shifting our gaze, we examine the shadows and still see plenty of detail. The eye adjusts its aperture to make a good exposure on the brain. A light meter, whether built in or hand held, performs the same function for the camera that your eye does for your brain: it measures the light coming from the subject and suggests f-stop and shutter speed settings for the particular film speed.

Exposure	Amount of light to which the film is exposed.
Overexposure	Film has been exposed to too much light. Part of the picture is too light.
Underexposure	Film has been exposed to too little light. Part of the picture is too dark.

Unfortunately, no film can capture, in a single picture, the extremes of light and dark that the human eye can. Film can record details found in dark shadows or a subject set in bright light, but not both.

Consider, for example, a vase with a neck that flares out dramatically. To photograph it, we need to set it out in bright sunlight. It looks good through the lens: the top is lit as though it were in a spotlight, and the design element on the rim is easy to see. The exterior of the body is shaded by the rim, but the shade is uniform and the patterning is clear. Here are the metering choices:

- If the meter reading is taken off the top of the vase, all the neck detail will appear in the picture, but the body of the vessel will look as though it had been painted black.

- If the meter reading is taken from the body of the vessel instead, the color and exterior design will be captured, but any detail on top disappears into a big white splotch.

- If a meter reading is taken from both the top and the body and the exposure is set somewhere in between, an extremely faded design element on the top will appear in the picture (if it is discernible at all). The body will appear very dark with an inaccurate color that may mislead future analysts.

Don't blame your light meter. The film simply cannot record such variation in light. You'll need to move the vase into the shade to eliminate the contrast. To succeed in field photography, you'll have to rethink your definition of high contrast. For another example, see figure 2.1.

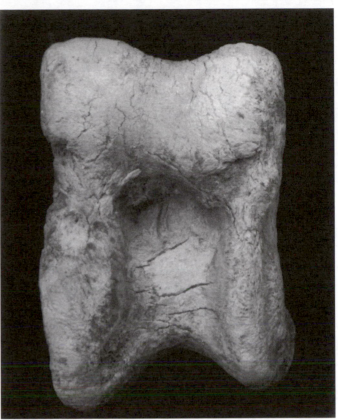

a   *b*

Color slide film can record only a very narrow range of light; it has a very narrow latitude. Color print film has a slightly greater latitude, and black-and-white film is more accommodating still. Any of these would, however, be hard-pressed to produce a good photograph of the vase in the sunlight.

WHAT YOUR LIGHT METER IS TRYING TO TELL YOU

The light meter is designed to do a specific job. Try as you might, you can't make it do anything other than what it was designed to do. When scanning a large black-and-white photograph, the light meter reads the scene (or any scene) by the amount of light the various parts reflect. It can take just a part of this scene—be it black, white, or any shade of gray—and tell you how to get a good exposure. What is meant by "good exposure"? It does not necessarily mean reproducing the shade of gray that it reads. If you take a meter reading from a dark part of the scene, the suggested camera setting will not reproduce this dark scene on the film. The recommended exposure will turn the dark gray into a more pleasing medium gray. In most situations, interpreting light for a medium exposure is fine. It can, for example, cause problems if the meter reading is from a dark textile. Because the meter recommends a medium-tone exposure, the picture is of a medium-colored, not dark, textile.

Because camera makers know their market well, the features of photographic equipment are oriented to the needs of the majority of camera users—people who want to take good pictures of other people. If you take a meter reading of someone sitting in the shadows, the meter first assesses the predominant light. On a scale from black to white, a face in the shadows

Figure 2.1 In direct sunlight, the highlights and shadows on this bison astralagus (a) are beginning to conceal information. Had this example been photographed with a color film, the contrast would even be more damaging. Moved into shade, the astralagus (b) can be photographed accurately because the contrast is reduced to a degree that the film can record.

Capturing Detail: Try to discover how much detail you can get in a close-up photograph of a brick wall. If you shoot the same picture at a 30th and a 60th, is there a difference in sharpness? Place a coffee mug (or other household artifact) on a high-contrast background and take a picture using a meter reading from the mug. Take another picture using a reading from a gray card. See how close you can get to the mug. Try several different f/stops to see the effect on the depth of field.

would be dark gray. To produce a good picture of this dark gray face, the meter suggests an exposure that will make the subject a little brighter than dark gray. On a scale from black to white, it suggests an exposure that is a medium gray.

If you meter a light-skinned person in very bright light, the recommended setting will give a slightly darker exposure so that the skin tones are good—that is, medium. The meter has no way of telling whether the subject is a face in bright sunlight or a light-colored textile. Its only job is to interpret light for a medium-tone picture.

To repeat, the meter is designed to read the light value of the subject and calculate the settings necessary to produce a medium exposure. This medium tone is at the *center* of the latitude of the film. By placing the subject in the center of this latitude, the film can still record details around the subject that may be somewhat lighter or darker.

Look at areas of your pictures that appear extremely light or dark. These areas reflected a degree of light that was too far removed from the subject. The latitude of the film could not capture the contrast. By recognizing how narrow the latitude is, compared with the range of light that we can see with our eye, we follow these precepts:

Be alert to high-contrast scenes. Whether you are dealing with a combination of bright lights and dark shadows—or a textile patterned with both very light and dark threads, recognize contrast as a potential problem.

Meter only the subject (the most important part) of the picture. You'll confuse the meter by reading too much of a dark background along with a light subject. The meter will think that the dark area is the subject. When a dark tone is placed right in the middle of the film's latitude, the subject, which is lighter, must be recorded as white.

Invest the extra time, effort, and film to take several different exposures. If important elements of the subject range from light to dark, all the detail can't be recorded in a single picture. Multiple exposures can capture some detail in the light area and some in the dark.

COMMON METERING PROBLEMS

Most light meters are *center weighted*; they read the light from an area in the middle 30 to 50 percent of the scene. The meter assumes that this is the location of the subject and that the subject will be at least this big. Now we'll look at some common problems that demonstrate instances when the meter operated successfully but the picture didn't accurately capture the subject or scene.

Not Reading the Subject

On the last day of a site survey, you come across a built-up stone marker that is overgrown with dark blackberry vines. Because you can't clear it and there is no time to investigate it further, you settle for a picture. When the picture is processed, it shows a bunch of medium green foliage with a whitish blotch in the middle.

Because most light meters read values from a very large area, they think the subject is about 50 percent of the scene and is at its center. The meter evaluates differing degrees of light on a proportional basis. To make sure that the predominant subject gets the best exposure, it is reproduced in a medium tone, which allows for its attendant highlights and shadows.

In this problem, 90 percent of the scene is dark foliage, and so the meter assumed that this was the part of the picture you were most interested in and recommended an exposure that reproduced it in medium tones with as much surrounding detail as possible. To turn that dark area into a medium tone, it added a lot of light, overexposing the stone marker as a result. Here are some techniques to try next time:

> *Make sure that the meter reads only the light from the subject.* If you can't get close, meter on something else that is of similar color and is in similar light or use a spot meter. A spot meter can read light from a very small area— which allows you to get a good exposure on a remote feature without scrambling up a hillside. Some cameras have a spot-metering capacity built in. This feature not only saves packing an extra piece of equipment, it also saves you about $300.

> *Be alert to contrasts in tone.* You know that bright sunlight and dark shadows are a problem. Less obvious high-contrast situations can also adversely influence metering. Consider the contrasts in tone if you are trying to photograph, for example, a piece of bone in a dark soil context or an interesting mortar used to set red bricks in a wall. If you simply cannot get an accurate meter reading of your subject (stone marker, bone, or mortar), remember that the average meter reading will bring the predominantly dark background (foliage, soil, or brick) up to medium tones.

> *To keep the background dark (and retain detail in lighter areas), underexpose the meter's recommendation.* If the meter says to shoot at f/8, try it. Then follow this exposure with one at f/11 and one at f/16—to reduce the light gradually. One exposure will be perfect, depending on the film and the degree of contrast between the subject and the background.

Extremely Light or Dark Subject

You have several pieces of white bone emerging from a very light-colored sandy grid. You want to photograph them in situ as the excavation progresses. Contrast is not a problem in this situation, and so you simply meter the grid and shoot. But your pictures appear to be documenting an excavation of yellowed bone from tan-colored sand. What happened to the color? Because meters evaluate the predominant light, they recommend an exposure that will capture this predominate subject in a medium tone on film. The meter reads this abundance of light and assumes that it is a face in bright sunlight. It reduces the exposure to reproduce the face in medium tones. Here are some techniques to try next time:

> *Overexpose anything that needs to be recorded in accurate light tones.* White snow, light sand, whitewashed architecture, light-gray stone structures, light-colored textiles, or anything else that you wish to record in accurate light tones needs to be overexposed. Because the meter suggests an exposure for a medium-tone picture, you have to add light to this recommended exposure by overexposing by one or two f-stops. Open the

Shading the Lens: To prevent sunlight from falling onto the lens, use a lens shade or shield it with your hand.

Selecting a Gray Card's Size: For any artifact smaller than 8½ by 11, a gray card that is 5½ by 8½ should suffice.

aperture by moving to a lower f-number or use a slower shutter speed. In our problem, a solution would be to take one exposure as the meter recommended (f/16 at a 250th), then make one at a 125th and a third at a 60th. One of these will be an excellent picture of the feature.

Underexpose anything that needs to be documented in accurate dark tones. Black cats, dark soil, dark wood structures, dark foliage, dark brick, dark colored textiles, or anything else that you wish to document in accurate dark tones needs to be underexposed. When you meter a dark subject, the meter suggests an exposure for a medium-tone picture. To capture the dark tone, reduce light by underexposing the meter's recommendation (close the aperture by moving to a higher f-stop or use a faster shutter speed).

I was once asked to photograph a plain-weave textile that was dyed black and that had a minor design element in red at the hem. The textile specialist on the dig felt that it might be a significant Inka wraparound dress. Definitive analysis would have to wait, and the piece had to be left in Peru. I didn't want an overexposed picture of a "gray" textile with an "orange" design. And, the piece had wrinkles in it that kept it from lying flat, causing it to reflect light unevenly. I took one exposure at the metered setting (which turned out too light), then reduced the light by half-stops. (Many camera lenses can be set at a position between normal f-stops, hence the term *half-stop*.) The third exposure captured the most information.

USING A GRAY CARD

A metering aid called a *gray card* is a piece of neutral gray cardboard (made by Kodak, Unicolor, and others) that reflects a specific amount of light. Used as an industry standard, its medium is the tone the light meter tries to achieve with its recommended exposure.

The back cover of this book is made to the specifications of a gray card. You can cut off all or part of it to keep in your camera case. It won't be as rigid as a purchased gray card, but you can increase its life expectancy by keeping it in an envelope with a stiff piece of cardboard. Protect it and keep it from bending because, should it retain a bend or curl, it will pick up stray light and throw off the meter reading.

With Artifacts

For pictures of artifacts, this simple tool will do more to improve the overall results than just about anything else. When you're setting up a picture, hold this card in front of the subject until you see plain gray through the lens. Meter the light on the card rather than on the artifact, and then set the f-stop and shutter speed.

A studio photographer might, for example, be asked to shoot a layout of a can of vegetable soup and all its ingredients. (What would you meter on?) When the scene is set, the photographer places a gray card in the scene so that it reflects the same light that is on the layout. A meter reading is taken from the gray card. With the exposure set for this medium tone, the tomato will be captured in a medium red on film, the onions stay light, and the bell peppers are dark. When read with an averaging meter, this same exposure would be influenced by any imbalance of light or dark tone. If there were more dark objects than light, the meter would add light to compensate. Among other things, this would make the medium-red tomato appear a rather underripe pink.

In a snapshot of a family picnic, it doesn't matter whether the bread in Uncle Fred's sandwich appears as white or whole wheat. For research data, on the other hand, recording such distinctions can be helpful, even essential, to interpretation. Whether whole-grain or ceramic temper, you can capture such textural information consistently by using a gray card.

Photographing artifacts on a black background is dangerous without a gray card. It is too easy to include too much background in the meter reading. Set up the artifact, get the camera in place, and then hold the gray card as if you were taking a picture of it instead of the artifact—*so that it reflects the same light as the artifact.* Set up the artifact on the black background; place the camera; hold the gray card up as if you were taking its picture; meter the card; set the camera from this reading; remove the card; and take the picture.

Any portion of the artifact that is this same medium tone is right in the center of the film's latitude. A light slip stays light, a dark design element stays dark, and the background is black as ink.

In an Emergency

These items will serve as a makeshift gray card when you have lost or left yours behind:

- A nonreflective brown paper bag or burlap sack will come within (about) one f-stop of being a gray card. Overexpose a reading taken from the bag by one f-stop.

- The palm of your hand is also a pretty good gray card. Again, overexpose the reading by one f-stop. Hold your hand in the same light as the subject, and get the camera close enough to make sure that the reading is only from your palm.

- In a dark, dense jungle or forest, the full exposure that the meter recommends will make the scene look like a sunny park. Find, if you can, a highlighted patch of green foliage and meter on this brighter tone to get a good neutral exposure—one that will capture the detail, yet retain the dark tones.

- On a clear day, in morning or afternoon sun, meter the dark blue sky *away* from the sun. Be sure not to include land or clouds, just dark blue sky. This is a good average exposure for anything in the sunlight: an overall view of a site or an architectural feature sitting on a hillside way over there; a stone-lined path running from here to the horizon in full sunlight; or any walking-around-the-city-with-your-camera-ready-be-cause-you-don't-know-what-you'll-see-next situation. Depth will be important. Set your f-stop at the smallest aperture (f/16 or 22), then meter the dark blue sky to determine shutter speed.

If your camera does not have completely automatic functions, prepare for the panic shot by setting this average exposure. You can follow up with a more considered approach if the opportunity permits.

Less light   More light

Lens f-stops

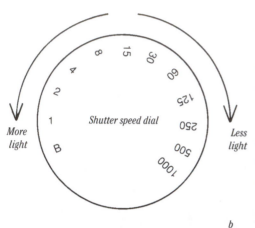

Shutter speed dial

More light

Less light

a

b

Figure 2.2 Lens f-stops (*a*) and shutter speeds (*b*) with more or less light.

Copying High-Contrast Graphics

If you have ever tried to photograph a black-on-white chart, graph, map, sign, title slide, illustration, diary, or document and the resulting photograph showed the item as black on gray, you may find a gray card helpful. When you metered from the high-contrast item, the meter read all the bright white background and then underexposed it for a nice medium tone. When you meter from a gray card instead of from the actual subject, you get a setting that will give a medium exposure for anything in the subject that is of medium tone. No part of a black-and-white subject is in this range. Both the black and the white are so far removed from this medium gray that they are beyond the latitude of the film and can only be reproduced in black and white.

If you need to replace your gray card (or you don't want to cut up this book), you can order one at a photo shop. (Some large camera stores keep them in stock.) A set of two neutral gray cards will cost about $10. In order of importance, this accessory ranks right next to film.

ADJUSTING THE EXPOSURE

Increase or decrease light by adjusting either the f-stop or the shutter speed (fig. 2.2). Shutter speeds are given in fractions of a second. F-stop numbers are in reverse order to aperture size; that is, a high number means a small aperture opening.

Some cameras have an exposure adjustment setting that reads +1, +2, -1, and so on. To add light to the metered exposure, use a +1 setting. Only your camera knows for sure if the adjustment is made in speed or f-stop. Automatic systems can work well even in problem situations if you take the time to get out your manual and learn how to:

Over- or underexpose the scene. If your camera doesn't have this +1 dial, you may have to adjust the ISO setting for the film to achieve a deliberate over- or underexposure. This method will work just fine, but you'll need to remind yourself to reset the ISO to its proper place once you've taken the picture.

Meter on one thing, then use this reading to take a picture of something else. This will let you use a gray card, or get right up to a subject in a high-contrast setting. You meter the subject, back away, and take the picture.

FILM LATITUDE

Film is sensitive to minor variations in light as it records a detailed image. The threads in a textile show up because the film distinguishes between the bright light on top of a thread and the darker tones on each side. The range of dark to light in which the film can make such subtle distinctions is called its *latitude*. The range is narrow, much more limited than what the eye can perceive. If the subject is in sunlight, we make an exposure for this light. The film recognizes slight variations in light to record the image. If a dark shadow cuts across part of the subject, the film cannot record detail in this area because the degree of darkness exceeds the latitude of the film. The photograph will be black in this area.

Latitude varies slightly according to film type. Generally, with color slide film, any part of the scene that is two or more f-stops away from the metered exposure will be so dark or light that most detail will be lost.

When taking a meter reading from a dark subject, place the tone of the subject in the middle of the available latitude so that it will be recorded in a medium tone. Only those things in the picture that are close to this subject in tone (within two f-stops) will be recorded with good detail. Anything that is much lighter than the subject is beyond the latitude of the film. This extreme light will come out white in the photograph.

METERING PITFALLS

Understanding the limits of a film's latitude will help you to recognize when an important part of the picture may be outside this range. For instance, for a subject that is a textile woven in shades of brown and black, some of the options and results are:

- If only the textile is metered, the recommended exposure will give medium tones to this dark subject. To compensate, I deliberately underexpose the meter's recommendation—reducing light so that the dark subject stays dark.

- If you meter on a gray card, the tone of the dark textile could be so far away from this medium gray (more than two f-stops) that the film will see only black—a problem with contrast. To get detail in the dark area, take a second or third exposure, adding light gradually.

Weavers seldom consider film latitude when they select thread color for a design element. A white design within an otherwise dark fabric is easy to overexpose. Textile analysts want to see those threads; you won't impress them with a white blotch. When metered from a gray card, white or very light-colored threads will exceed the latitude of a film, and details will fade into plain white. In such a case, follow the first gray card exposure with one or two exposures that gradually reduce light.

The progress of an excavation dictates when photographs must be taken. When it is time to add to the sequence of a feature as it is uncovered, to photograph a wall profile at a new level, or to get closing profiles before backfilling, these things must be done. Rest assured, the light will be terrible. Both bright sunlight and dark shadow will manage to fall on your subject. Two mistakes are often made in this situation: failing to get an accurate meter reading from the most important part of the picture and losing information by not allowing for contrast.

If you are lucky and have a feature in just sunlight or just shadow, get close enough to it so that the meter reading is only from the subject. Get close, take the reading, and then back up for the photograph.

For a floor or wall that runs from bright light to dark shadow, don't expect to get the information in just one photograph. Often, you can meter just the light area, back off, and shoot the grid with this exposure. Then, meter only the shadowed area, back off again, and shoot the entire grid.

The light falling on a profile is often mottled with highlight and shadow. To allow for both extremes, I get an average exposure of the entire wall for my first picture and then take two more pictures, one that is a full stop overexposure and one that is a full stop underexposure. When the light is harsh and contrast is high, this series of three exposures will always produce a more complete record.

Checking the Negative: Before blaming the meter for a poor exposure, look at the negative. If there is recognizable detail in the negative that got lost in the printing process, have it reprinted. The machines that print pictures produce an averaged exposure and may over- or underexpose an important part. Tell the printer which part of the picture is most important.

Photographs will never replace a good illustration of a profile, but they can confirm or add information or permit the illustrator to complete the work at a later time. They don't have to be pretty, but they do need all the detail available in a good exposure. For important closing shots or for an artifact that is about to be lifted out, this multiple-exposure routine will ensure that you get a complete record.

BRACKETING EXPOSURES

Bracketing is a term used to describe the practice of taking several exposures of the same scene. It takes very little time or thought and not all that much extra film. Professional photographers always bracket a chosen exposure simply because they have to come home with good pictures—and now you can, too. It is a good habit to cultivate for several reasons. First, people are inclined to make mistakes. They set the wrong film speed, fail to recognize a problem with high contrast, or work with weak batteries that give incorrect meter readings. Second, it is not always possible to guess which part of the subject is best to use for the meter reading. Third, the research process is destructive, and therefore a complete collection of data is essential. Finally, the significance of a feature may not be obvious at the time a picture is taken. In the field, you are in no position to judge the importance of something in the shadows.

Perhaps you don't believe in insurance, and wasted film means wasted money on a tight research budget. Let's try to put all of that so-called wasted film into perspective by considering the training, expertise, and research effort that went into the development of a field plan; the money invested in field equipment, travel expense, new tennis shoes, and camera equipment; the time, effort, and financial sacrifices of the other members of the team; the ethical standard that requires a researcher to do the best job possible; and the fact that, after a couple of weeks in the field, you will most likely have spent $150 on film and processing for a success rate of 50 to 60 percent. (Be honest with yourself: how many prints do you routinely shuffle to the bottom of the stack?) With a $200 budget, you might achieve a success rate of 95 percent. After all, you wouldn't write half a report to save paper, would you?

Although a professional photographer will say so, film is not cheap. Processing is not cheap. Camera equipment is not cheap. Fieldwork is not cheap. The failure to document fieldwork thoroughly and accurately is, however, very costly.

After evaluating the photos from your next field season, you'll find that the amount of information lost because of inappropriate exposures is apparent. I have about a 98 percent success rate with the photographs I am asked to take in the field. That does not mean I discard only two out of every one hundred photos. It means that I take enough pictures and bracket enough exposures that I can edit out fifty. The 98 percent of the remaining will be exactly what the project leader needs. The cost of the extra film is a small price to pay.

Note: All prices are estimates.

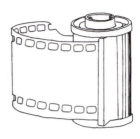

Chapter Three

Choosing Film

A s 35mm photography becomes increasingly popular, film manufacturers are introducing many new products. Most of the new
films are designed for amateurs interested in getting good snapshots. The colors are pretty and the print is sharp enough to pass around
without much explanation. For the archaeological researcher, vividness of
color is secondary to accuracy of color. Because researchers are also
concerned with recording minute details, we need a high-resolution film so
that an image of a textile, for example, can be enlarged and its threads
counted. The long-term stability of a film is also an important concern, given
that we want to make sure that the photo record survives as part of the
project archives.

CHARACTERISTICS OF FILM

Speed, resolution, stability, and color reproduction are the characteristics
of film. From the available choices, we select the ones that meet our needs
as researchers. And we arm ourselves with enough information to spot an
improvement when it comes along.

Speed

The speed of a film is indicated by its ISO (formerly ASA) rating. The ISO
number is always shown on the film box and may also be part of the brand
name: Agfapan 100, Fujicolor 200, or Kodachrome 25, for example. If your
camera is more than a couple of years old, the dial you use to set the film
speed may say ASA. (ISO and ASA are interchangeable terms, ASA being the
old American standard, ISO the now-uniform international standard.) Use
the ISO rating on the package. Many cameras now on the market can read the
ISO from a bar code on the film can, eliminating the need for setting the speed
manually and therefore the common mistake of forgetting to set it.

The ISO rate is determined by the film's sensitivity to light. A film that is
extremely sensitive to light needs only a small amount of light to record an
image and is called a *fast* film. Since it takes less light to get a good exposure,
you can use fast shutter speeds. A sports photographer may need a fast
shutter speed to freeze action. A journalist may select a fast film to use
indoors without a conspicuous flash; however, this versatility may require
us to settle for a poor-quality image (see "Resolution" below).

The most commonly used range is between ISO 25 and 1600 (see table 3.1).

Table 3.1 Fast, medium, and slow film speeds.

slow	25 to 64
medium	100 to 200
fast	400 to 1600

Table 3.2 Film speed and f-stop.

ISO	Variation in f-stop
64 *versus* 100	½ stop
200 *versus* 400	1 stop
100 *versus* 400	2 stops

Reciprocity and film speeds: Film speeds are relative and fit right into the reciprocal arrangement of shutter speed and f-stop. Suppose that two cameras are set up to take the same picture at the same shutter speed. If one is loaded with ISO 100 film and the other with 200, there will be a one stop difference in the f-stop. The 100 film needs more light to get the same exposure, and so it must be set at one f-stop lower than the 200 film.

Every time a film speed is halved or doubled, the one-stop variation remains the same (see table 3.2). Adjusting the ISO setting is another way to get a deliberate over- or underexposure. To overexpose the picture, you would in essence tell the camera that you were using a slower film, one that needs more light to take this picture. If you had 100 film in the camera, you would reset the ISO to 50 to overexpose by one f-stop. *Use this technique with caution.* It is very easy to forget to reset the ISO to the correct speed.

Pushing a film: Many films can be used at a speed that is faster than their given ISO speed. Some photographers choose to do this if they feel they need a faster film than what is at hand. If we take a 400 film and set the ISO at 1600, we are "pushing" it two stops. Please note, however, that the *entire roll* must be shot at 1600, and the processor will have to use special care in the developing. If you feel you must resort to this technique, first make sure that the necessary processing is available. Kodak now offers special processing for Kodachrome 64 that has been pushed one and one-third stops and shot at ISO 170—but only 170. I don't recommend this practice for any film because this forced processing will degrade resolution.

Wrong ISO: When you have accidentally shot a whole roll of film at the wrong ISO setting, special processing may salvage your work. Mark the can with the setting that you used and tell the processor what you need when you drop the film off for developing.

Resolution

Resolution is the term used for the ability of a film to record fine detail. It is judged by how many lines per millimeter can be reproduced sharply. (As we have already discussed, the overall sharpness of the picture is also dependent on the quality of the lens and the choice of f-stop.) Maximum resolution is a characteristic of *slow* films. Generally, the lower the film speed the better the resolution and the sharper the image. Slow films can provide enough detail to identify a botanical specimen, copy a detailed map, analyze the construction of a textile, or distinguish among fine elements of a painted design. The correct interpretation of photographic data often depends on the capture of very small details.

Stability

Long-term stability must also be considered when choosing a film. Occasionally, there is a time lapse between fieldwork and publication (or follow-up)—with ten years being the average. (In "archaeologist years," long-term stability is really a short-term problem.) Make an ill-advised choice of film and your carefully taken photo record can simply self-destruct. You need to make sure that you use reliable film for these reasons:

- *An excavation is destructive.* The archaeologist must meet the ethical responsibility to preserve all data in the best manner possible.

- *A final report is seldom final.* The knowledge we apply to interpreting results is cumulative. As that knowledge increases, we serve both our project and the greater world of archaeology by maintaining a complete record for reevaluation. Photographs of sites taken more than one hundred years ago are still a source of information for working anthropologists.

A well-processed black-and-white negative (of any type) is the most stable resource. By taking care with storage, you can consider the image practically permanent. Among color films, Kodachrome is the only choice because Kodak addresses the archive concerns of research in the manufacturing and processing of this slide film. With limited handling and care in storage, Kodachrome offers the assurance of more than one hundred years of stability. No other film meets this criterion. In second place, with at least fifty years of stability, are Fujichrome, Agfachrome, and Ektachrome (E-6 processed) slide films. Color negatives may last only twenty-five years (American Society of Magazine Photographers 1984).

Professional Films: Do not pay a premium for the *professional* label on a film. This film is aged to peak color balance and needs to be kept refrigerated for stability. The manufacturer tests each lot of film and includes, if necessary, specifications for fine-tuning color balance. Adjustments to color balance are made by using gelatin filters, which are too fragile for fieldwork. The film should also be used and processed immediately. It just doesn't make sense to pack this film in the field. (Chapter 7 includes suggestions for some professional films you may want to try in your home studio.)

Color Reproduction

Film selected for field research must be able to record color accurately. Color is often an important element in the evaluation of data. When photographing artifacts that must be left in the field, I make sure that I don't skew future analysis with false (but perhaps pretty) colors. The analyst must have accurate colors.

Most photography, from family snapshots to magazine layouts, is enhanced by vivid color. As a result, most color films exaggerate reality a bit. Keeping up with how a new film handles color is a full-time task. Currently more than thirty different color slide films are available. Some will emphasize anything green in your picture, some give an added value to reds, and so on. Furthermore, the color balance of a particular brand of film will frequently vary by lot. Again, Kodachrome is a good choice because of its lack of a pronounced *color bias*. Kodak's efforts to limit the lot-to-lot variation in color balance makes this film popular with professionals and publishers.

Assuring accuracy with a color bar: You can include a color bar in a picture of a textile or ceramic so that the analyst can determine the exact color of a dye, paint, or paste. With a color bar, a printer can accurately reproduce a color even if the artifact is not available. Such fine analysis may not be needed very often. When it is, we can inhibit or mislead the analyst by omitting the color bar and having an exposure that is slightly off. A color bar takes up very little room and can be obtained at a photo supply store.

Even though most archaeologists are routinely concerned with the problems of interpreting photographs of cultural material and most are familiar with the use of color bars, very few researchers will use them. Even though their use could save hours of debate over whether a slip pigment is pink or lavender, two reasons are most frequently cited for not using color bars: to produce an aesthetically pleasing photograph for a presentation and to "fill the frame" with the subject to record more detail. After taking an

Using a Contact Print as a Map: I was once asked to locate a feature that had been photographed so many years ago that no one could remember its location. My "map" consisted of a contact print that had been pieced together from several rolls of film. I used negative numbers to determine which film strips might be consecutive and recognized a landmark a few frames away from my elusive feature. I could only hope that the landmark was photographed at about the same time. After hiking several miles to reestablish the view of the landmark, I was able to follow the photo trail back to the feature—a useful lesson on the value of having a roll of negatives to keep data in context.

aesthetically pleasing and full-frame photograph of an artifact, you can further document it by taking a second picture that reduces the image size and includes a color bar. For small items that require a close-up form that will not accommodate a color bar, retake three or four such items in a single frame with a color bar. For several items to be photographed in similar light, you could also take one picture of the color bar itself with the same light and exposure in order to provide the printer or analyst with the necessary information on color separation. If you must shoot an item without a color bar, I recommend using Kodachrome 64 because of its lack of color bias. If you take a well-exposed picture of a faded red textile with this film, you will not get a rich, glowing red but a faded red—boring, but reliable.

Note: Have negatives printed on a glossy finished paper. Detail can be obscured by matte or silk finishes.

APPLYING FILM TO TASK

What type of film is best: color slides, color prints, or black and white? It is expensive to have prints made from slides and more expensive to have slides made from prints. Black-and-white processing used to be cheaper than color. A finished roll of color slides will cost considerably less than either black-and-white or color prints. Some manufacturers offer both slides and prints from a roll of film, but don't waste your time and money. Neither the prints nor the slides will be acceptable for documenting research.

Do consider the primary use when selecting a film type. The best prints come from an original negative, the best slide is an original, and the best (and least expensive) duplicate slide is the second one that was taken in the field.

BLACK-AND-WHITE FILM

Because of its reliability and durability, black-and-white film meets our goal of preserving the best record possible. If you have a spare camera in the field, consider keeping it loaded with black-and-white film. Otherwise, plan to use a roll when you are between rolls of color film.

Working with black-and-white film takes some special effort. When you view a scene, for example, try to let all the color run out. Taking several practice rolls will help you learn how to evaluate a subject in terms of light and shadow. Without pretty colors to add interest, composition becomes essential. Keep your scenes as uncluttered as possible. And, attach a reminder to the back of your camera so that you'll remember you are using black-and-white film.

Contact Print

A contact print is a single eight-by-ten print (and some labs can prepare contact prints that are nearly twice as large) with a whole roll of film laid out on it (fig. 3.1). The pictures are the size of the negatives. After you have taken the roll of film for the project record, ask the processor for a contact print. Then, identify and store the negatives as a permanent part of the project record. (Individual prints can be made later if needed.)

If you photograph artifacts on print film, a contact print can be cut up into small pictures for attaching to the catalog description, which may be all the printing you need until a researcher or publisher requests an

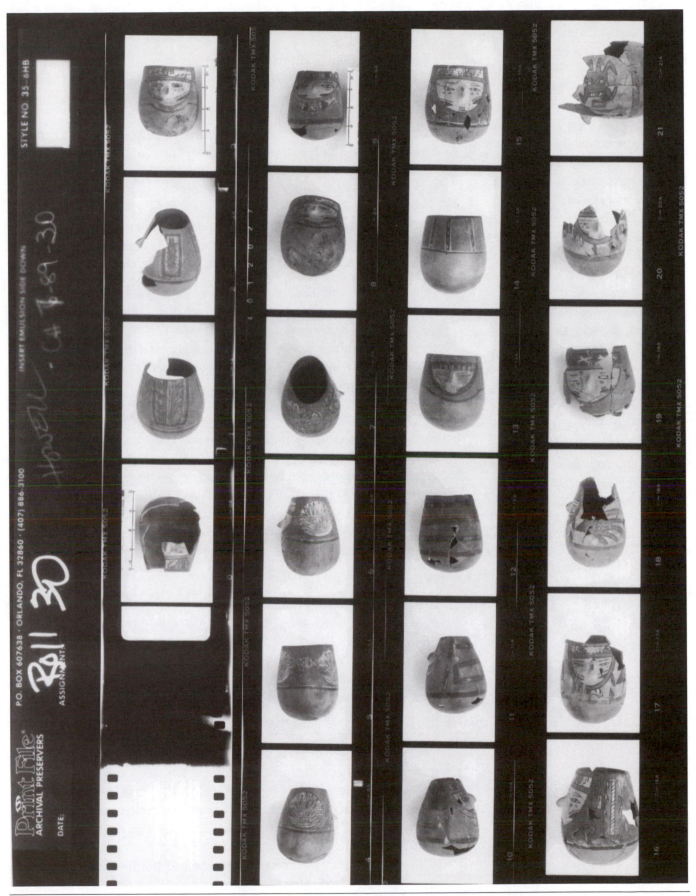

Figure 3.1 The contact print produces a small-format image of an artifact that can easily be attached to a catalog sheet. A contact print can also be used for creating a small map of a site (see figure 5.1).

Photocopying a Print: You can include a good representation of a site, feature, or artifact in a photocopied report with a black-and-white picture if you follow these guidelines:

Keep the scene simple. For a site or feature, try to eliminate a confusing background. Artifacts should be photographed against a white background so that the copy can be trimmed to fit the text.

Use a glossy finished print. Silk or matte finishes do not copy as well. A black-and-white print seems to give more predictable results than color, but don't hesitate to try just about anything.

Customize reproduction by enlarging, reducing, lightening, darkening, or cropping the copy. Take a pair of scissors to any nonessential parts of the copy, fill in any faded details with a pencil, or add highlights to dark areas with an eraser. Then paste it onto the page of text.

This method will not replace professional printing but, with a suitable picture, it can be a good way to distribute information at a minimal cost.

enlargement. The picture will not be archive quality, but it is not your original; the negative is.

Aside from the advantage of having a comprehensive photo record in the archives, a strip of negatives retains information on relationships, one frame to the next. This can be essential to a future investigator who is trying to reconstruct who, what, where, and so forth.

If you have carefully bracketed an artifact or a feature, you can save money by asking for "processing and contact print only" because you use it to choose the best exposures for enlargement. When requesting enlargement, be sure to bring along the contact sheet for the printer to use as a guide for reproducing the particular exposure.

The cost of processing and having a contact print made is about half the expense of individual prints. The price of getting a contact print made from a file negative is even less.

Note: All processing labs are not the same. The amount of care that is taken in handling your film is critical and will vary dramatically from lab to lab. A good way to find the best local lab is to phone a couple of photo studios for their recommendation. A good lab will not necessarily be any more expensive than the stand that guarantees to develop your film in under an hour or your money back.

Publishing

Having some black-and-white photographs of your project can work to your favor with a publisher. Publishers love black and white because it has a greater latitude and captures more detail in very dark and very light areas; the film is thinner than the multilayered color film and produces a sharper image; black-and-white photographs are cheaper to print than color; and the print can be modified easily to retain detail in an overexposed area or to increase contrast.

In the Field

Use T-Max 100 for black-and-white photography in the field. It is a good choice for those who rely on commercial processing. Darkroom junkies may prefer Plus X, Ilford Pan F, or FP4, all of which are good choices for fieldwork.

Copy Film

A *copy film* produces a very high-resolution/high-contrast positive or negative image and is good for copying a line drawing or chart. Because the film has an exceedingly narrow latitude and it does not record gray tones, it will clean up a smudged drawing because it will not record smudges that are in this gray range. Copy films are useful for special tasks but are difficult to work with under normal field conditions (available light, wind, or chaos). You may have to use an ISO as low as 4, which means that the exposure will take you into next week. If you are off by more than a half stop, the results could be disastrous.

Copy films are not recommended for the field, but you don't need to have a controlled studio environment to use them. With patience, very bright sunlight, and careful metering, you can produce some very sharp graphics at home. In chapter 7, we discuss some choices for black-and-white and color film for graphics.

For copy work in the field, using Kodachrome 64 with a gray card is the practical alternative. You *can* copy a black-and-white subject with a color film. The fine detail in some maps may demand the resolution of Kodachrome 25; otherwise, Kodachrome 64 should suit most every subject. For a black-and-white print, Ilford Pan F 50 or T-Max 100 will do an excellent job of copying documents in the field.

COLOR FILM

Color adds information to the record. Of slides and prints, long-term stability favors slides. Professional outdoor photographers, who must meet a publisher's demand for high-resolution pictures, rely almost exclusively on these two films:

Fujichrome 50 Because this film emphasizes green, it is often used for scenes with a green subject (jungle, pastoral, or landscape). It also produces good skin tones. Choose either 50 or 100 for use during travel related to field research, when concern for archiving is not primary.

Kodachrome 64 Because of its lack of pronounced color bias as well as a limited variation in color balance from lot to lot, use this film for everything else. Printers love its no-gimmick consistency. With its outstanding resolution and archive quality, this film is the first choice for fieldwork.

Duplicating Slides

When duplicating slides, most processors use Ektachrome or Fujichrome. These films stand up to the rigors of projection, but they will not be as sharp as the original. The process can also cause a color shift and an increase in contrast (which may be an advantage). Some labs can color-correct a slide that was taken under fluorescent light and has that sick green cast. Because duplicating is done by people, it can, however, be done very poorly. If the results are unacceptable, have the processor try again or try another lab.

Note: See appendix D for tips on film choices for slide presentations.

Maximum Resolution

Kodachrome 25 has the finest resolution available in a color slide film. For the average photo of fieldwork or artifact, however, there is little difference between Kodachrome 25 and 64. Kodachrome 25 will make a difference when you must reproduce a very fine line. The added resolution can be necessary for copying a map or illustration that has been drawn with close fine lines or for showing a yarn plied with an S or a Z twist. When resolution becomes this important, review the checklist in chapter 8. Unless you use Kodachrome 25 with very good technique, however, the advantage is lost.

Making "Duplicates" in the Field: As you take a picture, you may catch yourself thinking "wait till they see this." This is the time to take two or three shots of the same scene. These extras will be your best-quality "duplicates" at about half of the cost and none of the wait.

Prints for Display: Taking a spectacular print for display purposes requires extra effort. Use all the techniques you can for getting a sharp image: bracket your exposure and use a small aperture and a tripod. Wait for light that lends itself to polarizing (mid-morning or mid-afternoon) and use a good polarizing filter to get rich colors (see chapter 4).

The first choice in film is Ektar 25 because it has the best resolution of any color print film. With a very good camera lens, you can get an excellent sixteen-by-twenty print. Even a medium quality lens will produce a knockout eleven-by-fourteen print. The Ektar films have a narrower latitude than other color print films, and so they are easy to over- or underexpose—bracketing is a must. The second choice is a tossup: Fujicolor 100, Kodacolor 100, and the higher-contrast Ektar 125 are all print films. Or have a print made from a very sharp slide. A print from a negative will be less expensive. All of these should enlarge well to at least eleven by fourteen.

If you are on an expense account, try getting a Cibachrome print made from a good slide or negative. The colors will be vivid and the image resists fading. Check the yellow pages for a photo finisher that does Cibachrome printing. If you are on a budget, the cheapest print from a slide is a direct R-type. This print will lack the very sharp resolution of one made from an Ektar 25 negative or a Cibachrome, but an eleven-by-fourteen print from a slide may be good enough to meet your needs. To get a good sixteen-by-twenty print from a slide, you'll need to have a four-by-five internegative made first, and then have a sixteen-by-twenty print made from the negative.

Publishing

Printing photographs is expensive for a publisher, and color is more costly to reproduce than black and white. Usually, the author needs to sell the idea. If your article is accompanied by good photos on Kodachrome 64, your sales pitch has a greater chance of succeeding. It is a publisher's only choice for color reproduction.

Prints

Color print film is useful to the researcher who wants to work away from the slide projector. The format lends itself to in-depth study, comparison, and review. For example,

- For examining a design element around a vessel, you can set three or four photographs side by side.

- For a drawing of a mural or petroglyph, take a variety of views, lighting, and close-ups to help an illustrator complete work after the field season is over.

- For a comparative study of similar artifacts that may involve several references in different locations, prints are convenient.

- For the analysis of a textile, an ordered sequence (overall, one half, other half, close-ups) is helpful, including close-ups that show selvages, frays, tears, any variation in weave, design elements, seams, or repairs. With good notes on your observations, an analyst can lay out the textile from your prints and give detailed information on the technology it represents.

In the midst of fieldwork, it's unlikely that any of these uses will be anticipated, but it can be worthwhile because prints made from a high-resolution negative film are sharper than those from a slide. Print film also has a greater latitude than slide film, and so it can record more detail in highlight and shadow. Because of the long-term instability of color print film, such an artifact should also be photographed on Kodachrome 64.

Pack a couple of 24-exposure rolls of Kodacolor Gold 100 for use when you come across an item whose meaning may require time, a reference book or two, or a specialist to resolve. To reduce processing expense, have only a contact print made and then request glossy enlargements of only the best photos.

When you are seeking the expertise of others, you can improve your odds of getting a reply by providing sharp five-by-seven glossy prints so that your specialist will not have to set up a slide projector to view your pictures.

FILM FOR INDOOR USE

The worst photographs any archaeologist takes are usually those shot in a museum—but it has more to do with the setting than the photographer. For example,

- Light may be coming from a window, a tungsten bulb, a fluorescent tube, or a combination of these—all of which change the color of the artifact.

- Light is normally dim, requiring slow shutter speeds, and some museums have rules against using a tripod without special permission.

- An artifact is often lit from only one direction, which creates very high contrast overall and loses detail in highlight or shadow.

- Metering is usually thrown off by whatever background the artifact is on—and access to the artifact is limited.

Solving any of these problems means we must plan our attack and make choices (and sacrifices) based on our goals.

Tungsten Film

Recording the color of an artifact accurately is often the most difficult problem. Ektachrome 160 tungsten film gives good color under incandescent light (that is, the round light bulbs used in most homes), but not fluorescent.

Filters for Artificial Light

Daylight film is any film that would normally be used outdoors. It can be used with a filter to correct for either tungsten or fluorescent light. The drawback is that adding filters reduces light (as much as two and two-thirds f-stops) and slows shutter speeds. The sacrifice may be futile under fluorescent lighting because there are six types of fluorescent light, each of which calls for a specific filter to get an accurate correction. Using an FL-D filter may be the best solution (see chapter 4).

Invest in a collapsible monopod if you frequent museums. A tripod or monopod may also be necessary if you wish to use a filter. Otherwise, the information that you lose by having to shoot at the lowest f-stop will probably not be worth the improvement in color. When you have a slide duplicated, the processor may be able to correct the greenish cast caused by fluorescent light. If your hand is steady, you may wish to try a filter with one of the faster daylight films noted below. Use these techniques to color correct a daylight film:

- For tungsten light, use an 80A filter.

- For fluorescent light, use an FL-D filter.

- For fluorescent lighting, see Kodak's filter specifications for specific shades at a retailer.

Fast Film

Fast films reduce resolution, but they may give better results than a slow shutter speed and a large aperture. Two of the best color slide films that combine speed and sharpness are Ektachrome 200 and Fujichrome 400. For resolution, these two beat out others of comparable speed.

Ektar 1000 (color print film) has a narrow latitude that works best when the subject is in uniform light. The slightest over- or underexposure is a problem, and so it's not useful for photographing in museums.

Increased Latitude with Slides: Some labs offer *reverse processing* for black-and-white film, producing a slide (positive) rather than a negative. What is gained is that the increased latitude of black and white retains details in areas that a color film would over- or underexpose.

This process can produce some very good pictures of museum interiors. Showcase light creates bright highlights and dark shadows on artifacts. It is beyond the latitude of a film to capture detail at both extremes, but black-and-white film will record more than color. Colors are so distorted under artificial light that little is lost by using black and white.

Kodak's T-Max 100 and Ilford Pan-F can be specially processed to produce a slide (positive image) rather than a negative. Reverse-processing kits are available for those who do their own processing. You'll need to find a lab that offers this special handling—generally small, independent ones. Ask them to suggest a film with which they have the most experience.

BLACK-AND-WHITE VERSUS COLOR

Black-and-white film can sometimes give outstanding results in museum settings. Its increased latitude has a distinct advantage in capturing detail. If prints will meet your needs, use T-Max 400 for both speed and resolution. You can rephotograph an important print to get a slide, or you may wish to try one of the black-and-white slide techniques noted earlier. Even though it's a sacrifice, no color may be better than bad color.

INFRARED

Because of its inherent inconsistency, infrared film removes itself from the set of reliable research tools. It certainly is not suited to remote fieldwork, given that it requires refrigeration, absolute darkness for loading and unloading the camera, and immediate processing. Any heat, including body heat, will fog the image.

Suppliers do not come right out and tell you what ISO to use, but they will often make a few suggestions. There is a notable variation in light sensitivity from lot to lot, and so two rolls of the same lot should be purchased. One will be used as a test to determine the best exposure. After judging these results, the second roll can be shot, bracketing each exposure by half-stops. The light for the second roll must, of course, be the same as it was when you took the test roll.

James Grady, a photographer who specializes in aerial photography of archaeological sites, says that it is seldom worth the effort and that he could often see more in a good black-and-white image than in an infrared one. If you are interested, see Kodak's *Applied Infrared Photography* for some vague suggestions on using this inconsistent film. If you ever run into anyone who has had repeated success with this film, find out everything you can and write it down.

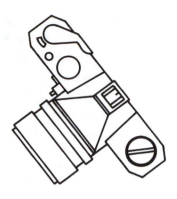

Chapter Four

Camera Accessories

*E*ach of us must decide how much equipment to carry. When selecting accessories, I make a photographer's distinction between technically good and excellent photographs. When I must pack my accessories on a two-mile hike in the desert, however, I have been known to make sacrifices in technical excellence. In harsh field conditions, good photographs can meet the goal of collecting accurate data. "Good" may be the best possible, or whatever you decide is good enough.

My suggestions are based on weight, how much I can handle in an airport, the accessories that have been useful in the field, and those I have packed and never used. First, we'll discuss accessories for general field photography and then special equipment for close-up projects.

CAMERA CASES

Bags designed for holding cameras and lenses come hard- or soft-sided. A hard case will better protect equipment from bumps, but a soft, padded bag can be better suited for travel and is easier on the hips. A narrow briefcase shape rides close to the body and is convenient in airports and unfamiliar places. A canvas exterior will get dirty and look grubby, which will make it less of a target for thieves. A handle that can be held firmly is als an antitheft device.

When loaded for travel, a bag can take a toll on the shoulders. Threading the shoulder strap through a piece of sheepskin can make the strap ride more comfortably.

UTILITY VESTS

A safari vest can be more than just a fashion statement in the field. Notebooks, pencils, tools, tapes, camera, lenses, film, filters, cable release, sable brush for lens cleaning, water, aspirin, bandages, sunscreen, tissues, gum, and lipstick add up to a lot of weight. Dropping all of this into a bag or backpack invites damage, inhibits access, discourages you from changing to a better lens or filter, and can ruin both your shoulders and your attitude by the end of the day. A vest with many pockets can help you keep everything accessible and distributes the weight evenly.

Cutting Atmospheric Haze: Atmospheric haze is more evident when shooting toward the sun. Use a UV or polarizing filter with color film to cut through the haze. For black-and-white film, you could also use a yellow filter. Do not, however, use more than one filter at a time.

Whether you use a vest or a sectioned pack, keep your tools organized, handy, and safely stowed. Once, as I watched an archaeologist make a quick change of lenses, he slipped the unused lens into his shirt pocket rather than into his pack. Unfortunately, he then bent over to inspect an ancient viaduct. He was able to recover his lens from the water, and it now makes a dandy paperweight.

When shopping for a vest, I looked at many that were made for photography or for fishing. Most were poorly sewn, made of a fabric that would tear easily or retain heat, were short on pockets, or did not have a pocket that would accommodate a telephoto lens. The photojournalist's vest sold at the Banana Republic clothing stores is a worthwhile investment, but it costs about $90. You could also try a local army surplus outlet.

LENS PROTECTION

In a wind or near an excavation, dust can cloud a lens quickly. A sable or camel's hair brush is the only cleaning tool I normally pack during the day. It will take care of dust on the lens or loose dirt on the body and will fit into a pencil pocket, keeping it clean and handy. A short-handled brush can be purchased in a cosmetic department, or you can cut the extra length off an art brush. You can't brush away fingerprints or a scratch; so, use a lens cap.

Caps and Bags

Lens caps can come and go, and when you have left one on a log a mile back, it's gone. I have never met anyone who actually carries a spare—people who do don't lose them in the first place. Camera stores sell a neat little gizmo for those of us who are ordinary mortals. It is a simple elastic band that slips around a lens, with a short cord that attaches to the lens cap. When you remove the cap to take a picture, it just hangs there until you are ready to put it back on.

Archaeology is a dirty business. An archaeologist I know dropped his extra lens into his canvas pack for a day's fieldwork. It now makes a crunching noise when it is focused because of the dirt under the focusing ring—and it will cost more to be cleaned than replaced. For about $5, you can get a little padded bag in which to store extra lenses.

Hoods

A lens hood is a sunshade that screws onto the end of the lens. It can be used with filters but not always with a lens cap. Most people who use a hood just leave it on the camera and leave the lens cap in the camera bag (or on a log). The hood will afford some protection to the lens, but not enough to justify its use in place of a lens cap—unless you are taking pictures all day.

Protecting the lens from direct sunlight when taking a picture is important. It is easy to use your hand to shade the end of the lens when the camera is on a tripod. With a little practice, you can learn to hand-hold the camera, shade the lens with one hand, and trip the shutter with the other.

I carry collapsible lens hoods but must admit that I use them in only about 20 percent of the situations that call for them—because I make a point of shading the lens by hand and because my lens manufacturer has taken great pains to coat the lens to reduce flare. Lenses will vary in the way that they handle direct light. If your results show a flare from sunlight hitting the lens, make sure that you use a lens hood.

Be sure also to use a larger, rectangular hood with a wide-angle lens, or the lens hood may cut off the corners of a picture.

When Not To Use a Filter: Lens optics perform best without any added filters. When resolution is critical, don't forget to remove protective UV or skylight filters.

FILTERS

Providing a simple way to improve a picture, filters can reduce haze, bring out important color, and selectively emphasize or separate tones. They can't do anything, however, if you do not take a moment to get them out and use them. Many garage sales are well stocked with expensive, unused sets of filters. The most practical approach to incorporating a filter into your routine would be to evaluate need carefully, buy one good quality ground-glass filter to meet that need, keep it with you, and take the time to use it.

Filters should not be used if they are scratched or dirty. There are some good plastic filters on the market, but, careful as I am, I have scratched every one I have taken into the field. Invest in a good ground-glass filter (for about $15)—and take the time to use it.

For Protecting the Lens

It is always a good idea to keep an ultraviolet (UV) filter on your lens. It won't affect your pictures, but it does protect the lens from the bumps and dirt of fieldwork. Remove it when using other filters or when resolution becomes critical. The UV filter is particularly useful at high altitudes. It reduces the predominant blue tone that is characteristic of intense ultraviolet light.

A skylight filter can also be used to protect the lens. It has a slight effect on colors and tends to add a brown tone. If you are using a skylight filter now, don't replace it; but if you do not have any filter to protect the lens, get a UV.

For Polarizing

A polarizing filter can cut down reflected light from particles in the atmosphere to reduce haze, and it produces dark blue skies and white clouds. It also cuts the reflected glare from many other surfaces, permitting you to capture the true colors of murals, botanical specimens, and geological features. A polarizer is a round filter that you turn to the point that is most effective. Watch for reflections to disappear or for the sky to turn dark blue, then meter and take the picture. Polarizing does not always work. It is most effective in mid-morning and mid-afternoon light (with the sun at a 45° angle over your right or left shoulder). It works well with both color and black-and-white films.

For Black-and-White Film

The only other filter considered by many to be basic for fieldwork is a yellow filter. Used by people who shoot a lot of black and white, a yellow filter will enhance contrast in most outdoor scenes, separating browns and greens, darkening blue sky, and highlighting clouds.

It may seem strange to use a colored filter with black-and-white film. The filter can, however, be used to block or lighten the parts of the picture that are of a similar color. It can be very successfully applied to specialized tasks such as copying a document that has yellowed with age. With the yellow

Advantages of a Using a Tripod: A tripod allows you to use very small apertures (high f-stops) for maximum depth of field, so that the area of sharpness extends from foreground to horizon in a landscape or over the entire surface of an artifact.

lightened, contrast is increased and better detail is captured. If, for example, someone has drawn over a map with red ink, using a red filter and black-and-white film should make it disappear.

TRIPODS

Using slower films and good technique often means using a tripod and cable release. More often than not, the logistics of a remote site survey leave little time for field evaluation of a site or artifacts. Best intentions aside, photographs must be taken with the attitude that follow-up could be years in the offing and might be done by persons other than the initial survey team. In remote situations, the researcher should be prepared to deal with a wide range of possible conditions:

- Dim light of late afternoon or heavy overcast

- Buffeting wind that jars both your body and your tripod

- Shelter interior that requires a lengthy exposure

- Limited perspectives that require maximum depth of field

Carrying a tripod is worth the effort. I have worked with many tripods in hopes of finding the perfect one for backpacking: one that weighs three ounces, folds into a pocket, stands rock steady in a strong wind, extends to five and a half feet, is flexible enough to plant on a steep slope, is not going to be damaged by sand or moisture, and can take the abuse I inflict while scrambling up and down a mountain side. I finally found one that meets all my criteria—except weight and size. Because a lightweight tripod can vibrate with any touch, as you walk around it, or in a gentle wind, mine is heavy and inconvenient to carry. Yet, I find it as indispensable as lens and film. The best brands of tripod for use in the field are Bogen, Slik, and Gitzo. The low-end Bogen costs about $100 and does a superb job (this is the one I use). The top-end Gitzo is a beautiful piece of equipment and a little easier to pack, but much more expensive. In cost and usefulness, Slik tripods are in the middle between these two.

CABLE RELEASES

One end of a cable release screws into the shutter button. By pressing on the other end, you can take a picture without having to touch the camera. Used when the camera is mounted on a tripod, the camera release reduces the possibility of camera movement. You'll need one that is at least about eighteen inches, which allows plenty of slack in the cable to avoid accidental tugs. (If you misplace your release, you can also use the self-timer built into the camera.)

REMOTE TRIGGERS

If you wish to mount your camera on a scaffolding over an excavation, you'll need a triggering device. One is a cable release that is about ten feet long. It has a bulb on one end; you squeeze the bulb to depress the shutter. It is also cheap. The other choice is an electronic trigger. A small device on the shutter button is activated by the push-button you hold in your hand.

STROBES AND REMOTE CORDS

Strobe and *flash* are terms used interchangeably. *Strobe* is used to distinguish the rechargeable electronic units from the older flash bulbs. A strobe can be a useful tool to lighten the dark shadows in a grid (reducing contrast) or to add oblique light across an incised feature (increasing contrast). Having a tested routine for the strobe lighting of artifacts to use when the elements demand indoor photography is also advantageous.

A remote cord lets you use the strobe off the camera. One end attaches to the camera where the strobe would normally be mounted; the other end connects to the strobe. You can hold the strobe yourself, have it held by an assistant, or secure it to a tripod in a position that gives the best light. (Other simple accessories for a field studio are detailed in chapter 6.)

Using a flash is never my first choice because I do not get to preview the effects and the results can be inconsistent. I have, however, used one during every field season—most often when I have a few hundred artifacts to photograph and a twenty-mile-an-hour wind outside.

There are too many possible combinations of cameras and strobes to try and run down exactly what you may need to get your flash to work off-camera. Your manual may give some clue, or take the camera and strobe to a large camera store. You may have to try a few places to find someone familiar with this accessory. Be sure to have fresh batteries in your unit so you can try the equipment in the store.

Some newer cameras will meter a flash exposure *through the lens* (TTL), which means that the camera, not the flash unit, meters the light and controls exposure. With this type of metering, the strobe can be placed anywhere.

If your camera does not have through-the-lens metering, light is metered by the strobe. The photographer reads from a dial on the strobe and controls the exposure by setting the f-stop according to the distance to the subject. When these are used with a remote cord, distance to the subject means the distance of the strobe to the subject. Distance of strobe to subject will vary with film type, the power of the strobe(s), and the f-stop you select. It is essential to use a roll or two of film to test this application before trying to use it in the field.

Keep a note with the flash unit to remind yourself to set the proper shutter speed on the camera—and to list other strobe and camera settings that have worked best. After testing for the best position of the flash with a remote cord, include reminders in your notes—for example, "with ASA 100 and f/16, place strobe no farther away than ten inches, at 45°."

After a picture is taken with a strobe, the unit needs a few seconds to recharge. When the indicator light says it is recharged for the next picture, wait a few seconds longer before firing it again. Many units will fire at less than a full recharge, causing an underexposure. After you have taken the last picture, let the unit recharge completely before turning it off.

Finally, take along plenty of batteries. When photographing many artifacts, I expect to replace a set of batteries every thirty-six exposures.

a *b*

Figure 4.1 (*this page and opposite*) This series of photos demonstrates how simple equipment can gather detailed information. The subject was in the shade and a tripod was used. Attention was given to keeping the camera parallel to the subject (with appropriate size scale and catalog number): (a) a standard 50mm lens set at its minimum focus, a distance of two feet; (b) 50mm macro lens that allows focus at a distance of one foot; (c) 105mm macro lens at minimum focus; and (d) 105mm macro lens with extension tube. Differences in thread ply are now discernible.

CLOSE-UP ACCESSORIES

Close-up photography requires patience and concentration and is technically demanding, but the results can be rewarding. There are many ways to get a close-up. You can use a macro (that is, close-up) lens, and you can use one of several accessories available for magnifying the image of a standard or macro lens. Beginning photographers sometimes take a mistaken approach to this specialty by first buying a close-up accessory. When the results are discouraging, the accessory sits in the closet. If you have tried one of the accessories listed below and were disappointed, get it out again and learn to use it. These are some of the requirements of good close-up photography:

> *Use a tripod and cable release to avoid the slightest camera movement.* Any shake will be exaggerated.
>
> *Use a high-resolution film to obtain the best detail.*
>
> *Focus carefully.* The depth of field is very small.

If you have met these requirements and resolution is still poor, the fault may be with the optical quality of your accessory or prime lens.

Macro Lenses

The term *macro lens* used to be reserved for lenses that could get a life-sized (1X) image unaided. Now, it simply refers to a lens that can focus close. Macro lenses provide high-quality resolution and an edge-to-edge sharp-

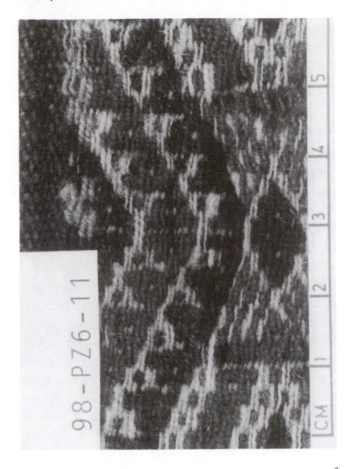

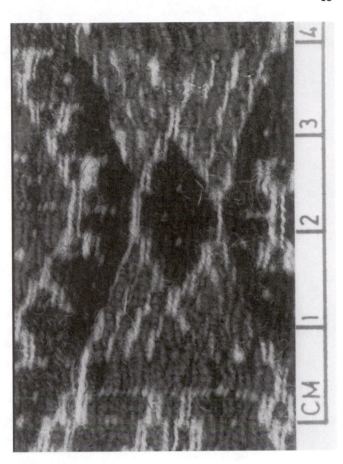

c   d

ness that cannot be obtained using a standard lens and accessories (fig. 4.1). They are the most convenient way to take a close-up and are perfectly suitable for distances as well. They are, however, expensive.

Extension Tubes

Extension tubes are simple rings that fit between the lens and camera, extending the lens and magnifying the image. A low-cost way to get a close-up, tubes are difficult to find now. Lens-to-camera connections have become more complex, and proper coupling is needed to retain automatic lens function. Extension tubes are useful because they do not add another thickness of glass and thus do not cut into resolution.

Bellows systems also extend the lens and have the advantage of controlling perspective, but they are not very practical for field use. Either system will give you one of the sharpest images possible up to a 1X magnification.

An automatic extension tube (Nikon is one of the few that makes them) is a good choice because it will give a sharp picture and is less prone to damage than lens accessories. If your lens can not work automatically with an extension tube, you will have to close the aperture manually before taking the picture. Although it is possible to work with a lens manually, you do run the risk of throwing off the focus when you close the aperture—or of forgetting to close it.

Long-extension tubes can be difficult to work with because they reduce light. At 1X or greater, the highest recommended f-stop is about f/8. Use the shortest extension tube you can. One that is 25mm in length on a standard

Motor-Driven Film Advance: Motor drives are for fast-action photography. They are also heavy, noisy, and prone to break.

50mm lens will give you about a .5X magnification. These extension tubes are also great on a telephoto lens (80mm to 105mm) and will allow you a more comfortable working space between camera and subject. If you go shopping for one, also check out the two-element Nikon plus (+) diopter before making any decision.

Two-Element Supplementary Lenses

Several manufacturers make two-element *plus diopter lenses*. This supplementary lens goes on the end of the lens like a filter and offers better resolution than a single-element close-up or magnifying filter. Most two-element lenses are corrected for a standard 50mm lens, which means you will be working very close to the subject. (When you must focus within inches, remember that it is easy to interfere with the light.)

Nikon makes an excellent plus diopter for longer lenses; it requires a 52mm or 62mm filter. (The size of a filter is found on the lens cap or on the filter itself.) This plus diopter lens comes in two different powers: +1.5 and +2.9. If your best lens is in the 50mm range, try the +2.9 diopter. With a good quality telephoto lens, the +1.5 diopter gives excellent image magnification.

These lenses start at $40 to $50, have minimal effect on the optics of the primary lens, are as easy to use as a filter, and allow you to use a telephoto lens at a comfortable working distance. They are the most exciting advance in close-up photography since the invention of the macro lens.

Single-Element Supplementary Lenses

Single-element supplementary lenses are also called *plus lenses*, close-up filters, or plus diopters; they attach to the primary lens like a filter. They are often sold in sets of varying magnification (+1, +2, +4, and so on). They don't interfere with automatic lens function, and they are low cost, portable, easy to use, and popular for taking close-ups. Optically, these lenses are not the best way to get a close-up, but if you have a set, try the lowest strength that meets your needs, use only one lens at a time, and use good technique. The results will probably be satisfactory. A sharp .25X image will most likely be more informative than a fuzzy .5X. Don't try stacking a set of these together—for a +8 combination. After seeing the results, you'll relegate the lenses to the closet. If you must stack them, place the higher power next to the prime lens and never use more than two.

Teleconverters

Like an extension tube, a teleconverter goes between the lens and the camera body. In addition to providing a larger image by extending the lens, it has a built-in plus diopter. Interfering with the lens's design to this extent can, however, create more problems than it solves. If you have one (or a set), give it another try before buying anything else. Teleconverters generally perform best with a lens set at f/8; consequently, some depth of field will be sacrificed. The subject should either be flat or have the element you are most interested in along a flat plane.

Reversing Rings

A simple and cheap reversing ring lets you mount your standard 50mm or wide-angle lens inside-out for an incredibly sharp magnification up to about

1X. These rings are the size of a filter without the glass, and most cost under $10. You will have to focus with the aperture open, then manually close it to around f/8 (at this range, the higher f-stops cannot resolve the image). Metering is done only after the aperture has been closed. If metering with anything but a dedicated lens loses anything, reversing is not for you. Depth of field barely exists at this magnification. If the subject is as three-dimensional as a kernel of popcorn, you will not get front-to-back sharpness. Even with all these potential drawbacks, you may still find it worth a try.

Coupling rings

With a cheap coupling ring (less than $10), you can use one lens as your "close-up" filter and attach it to another lens. With the right combination, a sharp 2X magnification is possible and also lets you retain all the automatic features of your prime lens. Zooms and macros may or may not work with this arrangement, but the two combinations of set-focal-length lenses shown in table 4.1 should do well.

Reversing and coupling rings are made by both Dotline and Kalt and may be available at a photo supply store or by mail order (see appendix C).

Fresnel Viewing Screens

A split-image focusing screen, on which two parts of the scene come together when you are in focus, is ill suited for most close-up work because you must often focus at a point other than dead center. A focusing screen with a shimmering (also called a Fresnel) view, which becomes sharp when the subject is in focus, is more useful. With this screen, you can position the camera and subject and then fine-tune the focus on the rim of a vessel if necessary.

Some Fresnel screens include a grid that helps to keep scales (and horizons) straight. This grid is also useful to keep a double exposure in a uniform position on each half of the picture. Your photo supply store will be able to tell you whether the viewing screen on your camera can be changed. Most models of Nikon, Canon, Olympus, and Pentax cameras can accommodate this screen, as will some others. It is inexpensive, and if, you don't like it, you can replace it with your old screen.

Note: All prices are estimates.

Table 4.1 Lens combinations.

Prime lens on camera	Added lens
200mm	80 or 105mm
135mm	35 or 50mm

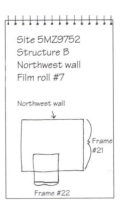

Chapter Five

Site 5MZ9752
Structure B
Northwest wall
Film roll #7

Northwest wall

Frame #21

Frame #22

Travel and Field Tips

Preparing for fieldwork requires deliberation. If you have never done any surveying, for example, it would be silly to take along a transit and hope for the best. If you do not have experience with the camera, accessories, or film you will be using, take some time to familiarize yourself with them. Having confidence in your equipment lets you devote your attention to the subject and makes picture taking more pleasurable.

BEFORE THE SEASON BEGINS

Taking your camera in regularly for routine maintenance is common sense. After all, it's a complex piece of equipment that is essential to documenting your project. For exactly the same reason that you change the oil in your car *before* the engine freezes up, make sure to have your camera serviced before you leave on a research trip.

Finding a good camera repair person is usually easy. What you need is good service, and good service is most often found in small, independent camera shops—ones that care whether or not customers return. It may be a business that specializes only in camera repair or that sells camera supplies and has a repair person in the store a couple of times a week.

About a month before you plan to use it, take the camera to be checked out—just in case any parts need to be ordered. Within a matter of minutes, a repair person can replace the battery, sell you a spare, check out the accuracy of the meter and shutter speeds, clean the camera up a bit, and make sure that it is in good working order. The cost will probably be little or nothing over the price of the batteries. You could return the favor by buying your accessories from this shop.

Avoid Super Duper Deluxe Camera Discounters. Sales people in such shops usually work on a sales commission, and repair service does not pay the rent. They may charge a handling fee for mailing your camera to someone who will charge you a teardown fee to look at it and then present you with an estimate for repair. Don't waste your money.

TRAVELING WITH FILM

Take along more fresh film than you could possibly use—do not even hope to get good film in another country (even if it is in a familiar yellow box). Because what you don't use in the field can be used at home, don't skimp. A roll for every day in the field is a sound estimate. Film can disappear quickly when you are photographing many artifacts, making sure to bracket your exposures, and taking duplicates. I have carried seventy-five rolls of film through airports. To save space, these were out of their boxes (but still in their plastic cans) and carried in ziplock-type bags. If the cans are not labeled, you can use colored adhesive dots (available at any office supply store) to indicate film type.

Make a point of allowing extra time for the airport security check so that you can ask for hand inspection of your film. On only one occasion have I had an inspector open each can of film. Fortunately, I was carrying only five rolls of film at the time.

The color shift induced by X rays is cumulative, and fast films are more likely to sustain damage. If a slow film is passed through an X ray once, the damage will probably be negligible, but don't risk it twice.

Fuji now uses a clear plastic can for its film, which could be a help with customs inspectors and security guards, but you will need to make sure that the film stays out of harsh light for the rest of the trip.

The lead-lined bags designed to protect film from X rays are heavy and bulky. If the X rays are moderate enough that the bag actually blocks them, the black image that shows up on the screen will cause the security people to check the bag anyway.

Suitcases often receive much more intense X rays than carry-on luggage does. So, packing your film is risky for that reason and also because you risk losing it along with your luggage.

DURING THE FIELD SEASON

As you settle into camp, find a spot in which to keep film and accessories, those items you will not be carrying in your camera bag every day. They should be out of traffic and dirt and organized for quick access.

At the end of a day of fieldwork, there are many chores to attend to, from completing the day's journal to preparing equipment for the next day. The routine should include updating photo logs, performing camera maintenance, and checking the film supply in your camera case.

Establishing a routine helps keep equipment clean and in good order. You can also refine your notes while the scenes are fresh in your mind. You can also circumvent a mistake, such as going into the field with two shots left in the camera and a bag full of already exposed film.

Caring for Film

Refrigerated storage of film is a good idea if it is available and if the film is left in the original, closed plastic container. When you take it out, let it warm to room temperature before opening the can and loading the film into your camera—to avoid problems with condensation. If you must do with room-temperature storage, make an effort to keep it under 70°F—the lower the better.

When you set out for a day of fieldwork or survey, carry only the film you expect to use that day—plus one extra roll.

Get exposed rolls out of your camera bag and into the coolest storage available. Carrying exposed film risks damage or loss. Or you can be misled into thinking you have plenty of film for the day, only to discover it is all exposed.

Protect film from heat, direct sunlight, excess humidity, and loose dirt (which may be rewound into the canister, scratching the film).When the camera bag is set aside for excavation, set it in the shade. To keep it out of the dirt and to take advantage of any cooling breeze, set up your tripod and hang equipment on it.

When you come to the end of a roll of film, rewind it back into the canister *slowly*. Rewinding rapidly can cause a buildup of static electricity that may leave a lightning-like mark across your film. This problem is especially acute in cold or dry climates.

When it is time to change film, find a spot of shade or shield the camera from direct sun with your body. Bright light can leak into film canisters. More importantly, should you open the back of the camera without having rewound the film, being in the shade will lessen the damage. Close the back *immediately*. If the exposure was very brief, you may only lose your last few pictures.

Resist the urge to donate your plastic film cans to the field lab and carry your film home naked. Cans provide the necessary insulation against rapid changes in temperature and humidity.

Dealing with Humidity

If you plan to spend longer than a week in a humid (averaging more than 60 percent) climate, take extra precautions with film. Even without heat, humidity can damage film by causing the emulsion to swell, layers to stick together, fungus to grow, and color to shift. When you have finished shooting a roll of film, dry the metal canister before resealing it in its plastic can. Silica gel is the most efficient desiccant available. Keep a small container of silica in a ziplock bag and toss in the exposed film to dry. Every few days during the less humid midday hours, again seal the dried-out canisters in their plastic cans. Even when the silica bags are not being used, keep them sealed or the silica will try to dry up the whole jungle. It cannot hurt to take the added precaution of storing film cans (fresh or exposed) in a ziplock bag with a little silica. Rice is a good substitute for silica. Bake it so it is dried out, let it cool in a sealed container, and then add film.

The camera should be put to bed in a similar silica-dry environment for both the film's and the camera's sake. I have used a hard suitcase with silica and had plenty of room to store cameras, lenses, and strobes. Any electronic equipment is at risk in this situation (for example, tape recorders, calculators, and radios). Silica can be purchased with a built-in indicator that turns various shades when it is saturated with moisture. Baking it in a 300°F oven for an hour or so will dry it out for reuse. (See appendix C for information on where to purchase silica.) Many hobby shops sell powdered silica for drying flowers—at less-expensive prices. You can repackage it into small cloth bags for field use. Since you won't be able to see the change in the indicator color, you'll need to remember to bake it every month. Handle silica powder

Figure 5.1 (*this page and opposite*) During this historical archaeology project, I took the time to wander around the site recording features and environment—because features can burn down and environments tend to get paved over. This contact print is part of the project records, along with the accompanying photo log that documents the views and orientations.

carefully because it is abrasive, and loose powder can damage camera and lens mechanics.

Photo Log

Many projects use $8\frac{1}{2}$-by-11 binders for uniform record keeping, but the size is impractical for use during the day. A simple pocket notebook, or the back few pages of a field journal, are convenient places to keep track of the pictures you take. A convenient format encourages you to take the extra notes and sketches that can be important. At the end of the day, this journal is copied onto a photo log. (Fig. 5.1 shows an example of a photo log and contact sheet used as a miniature site map.) Record the date, roll number, frame number, essential grid coordinates or artifact catalog number, and a brief description. It sounds complicated but, if you head the top of a page with the roll number and date, the entry for each frame could be as simple as:

> #14 [frame #], PV74-1-325-34 [cat. #], painted rim sherd.

Take a few seconds to jot down other observations because they can fade fast. Some information to add might include:

- Comments on an unusual paint or ceramic paste, or on vessel wear (or lack thereof).

- The direction you are facing when photographing a site or grid—for example, "Photographer facing N," "at center is S ext. wall of structure 2." Directions can be confusing. If you simply write "facing east," is the wall of the building facing east or are you facing east? Make it clear.

FOUR MILE HISTORIC PARK
Denver's Oldest Home in Cherry Creek Valley,
14-acre site to the south of Exposition and Cherry Streets
Date: July 27, 1989

1   Park Entrance on Exposition Street

2   Maintenance/Reception Building (modern).
     A corner of the Bee House should be visible just to the left of the Maint. Bldg.

3   Foreground: Bee House (N. & W. sides)
     Background: Four Mile House (NW Corner) & Privy (at Rt.)

4   Left: Bee House, Center: Four Mile House, Right: Privy (N. & W. sides)

5   Four Mile House (N. & W. sides)

6   Four Mile House (N. side)

7   Four Mile House (N. & E. sides)

8   Four Mile House (N. & E. sides)

9   Four Mile House (East side) "Front" of bldg. when it served as a
     stagecoach stop. Well is to the left.

10   Four Mile House (S. side). Well is to the right.

11   Dup. of frame 10, slightly broader angle of view.

<u>12</u>   Photographer Facing N.W.   <u>13</u>   Photographer Facing N.

CHERRY CREEK BUILDINGS   X BEE HOUSE   BEE HOUSE X   FOUR M·LE HOUSE
ROOT CELLAR   X PRIVY   PRIVY X
                             X CHICKEN COOP   CHICKEN COOP X   ROOT CELLAR

<u>14</u>   Facing E. (50mm lens)   <u>15</u>   Facing E. (telephoto lens)

ROOT CELLAR   X X X X X METRO ARCHAEOLOGICAL   ROOT CELLAR   X X X X X – ARCH. TEAM
                        TEAM ON HORIZON

<u>16</u>   Facing W. (telephoto)   <u>17</u>   Facing W. (telephoto)

CHERRY CREEK BUILDINGS   SURVEY CREW – CUTTING GRASS
ROOT CELLAR   FOR TRANSIT READING
                    METRO CREW SCREENING

<u>18</u>   Facing W. (telephoto)

                                                  CHERRY CREEK BLDGS
ROOT CELLAR   TRANSIT STATION
                                                  TRANSIT AT 20·25 E
               500 S.   LINE RUNS FROM O TO 243 E.

               O

- A sketch—if the picture is a view of three grids, for instance, show the relationship and identify each.

- A note of the time on two or three occasions during the day to help reconstruct sequences.

- The identity of any landmarks in a panoramic photo, such as the name of the peak on the horizon at 10 o'clock (or stream, church tower, or where the logging road leads).

- A note on the height of the wall even if the stadia rod appears perfectly legible.

Equipment Maintenance

A compact field repair kit includes the following items:

Camera manual

Cleaning solution for lens. For use on exterior lens surfaces, filters, viewing window, and any other camera body window that serves metering or viewing. If you are flying to your destination, wrap the solution in a paper towel and seal it in a small ziplock bag to ensure against leaks.

Cleaning tissue for lens. Chamois are popular but are about twenty times as bulky as a little pack of lens tissue. Also, we risk rubbing all the dirt and sand from the field into the lens when the chamois is reused. Use one clean tissue moistened with a few drops of solution to clean the exterior surface of a lens. Rub gently in a circular motion. Polish with a dry tissue. Repeat if any marks remain. Also check filters for fingerprints.

Sable or camel's hair brush. This brush is all that should be used on the mirror or interior lens surface. It is handy to have in the field to remove dust from a lens or filter. So, carrying two of these is a convenience. One stays with the maintenance kit; the other is kept with field equipment.

Rubber bulb-type air blower. This blower can be used to remove loose stuff from the camera interior.

Spare battery for camera

Masking tape. If you are out in the wind, a piece of tape over the hinge and seam of the camera back will keep out the grit. You can also wrap it around a stuck filter for a better grip when trying to loosen the filter. To keep things compact, wind a few yards of tape around an index card.

Pencil-shaped typewriter eraser with brush. The eraser cleans battery and strobe contacts (a common failure with strobes), and the stiff brush gets dirt out from under camera levers.

Cotton swabs. Moisten a swab with just a drop of lens cleaning solution, then squeeze out the excess half drop. Run the swab over fittings that connect the lens to the camera body to remove any grit.

Jeweler's screwdriver. This screwdriver can be used to keep various things tightly screwed.

It takes very few minutes to clean equipment in the evening, and the routine can prevent many problems.

When Something Sticks

When something sticks, something is wrong. *Do not force it.* Refer to the camera manual for any troubleshooting tips. Some possibilities include:

- Check to make sure that you are not trying to advance a roll of twenty-four exposures to number 25.

- Check the battery. Some cameras lock up tight when the battery is weak. If you can't get the shutter to release or the film to advance, the problem could be the battery, not mechanism.

- Check to see whether dirt could be interfering with the mechanics or electronics. Try rewinding the film. If you are in the middle of nowhere and unable to clean the camera, reloading may dislodge the dirt and solve the problem.

Opening a Camera Loaded with Film

When you cannot get the film unstuck or rewound, try to get it out so that you can check out the camera interior. You can make a dark room from a heavy coat that has been buttoned up and placed face down on a tabletop. Fold under the bottom, stick the camera on the inside through the neck, and then fold under the neck. For an added precaution, throw a blanket over all of it. Stick your arms inside through the coat sleeves, getting the sleeves to fit as tightly as possible.

Pop open the camera back, then try the release button and rewind lever again. If this still does not work, lift out the canister and free the exposed film from the camera. Holding the spool with one hand and the canister with the other, turn the spool to wind the film back into the canister.

After the film is safely rewound, try—gently—using a bulb-type blower on the interior, followed by a sable brush. Avoid touching the mirror or putting any pressure on the shutter. Even if you cannot see anything wrong, cleaning and reloading may solve the problem.

Avoiding Water Damage

Water and cameras do not mix. No picture is worth damaging your equipment. Remember that:

- Moisture will short out electronics.

- Salt spray causes almost instant corrosion.

- Moisture can creep into a lens, and fungus on the interior will ruin it.

Even with an umbrella or plastic camera "raincoat," the hazard is great. With irreplaceable equipment in a remote location, the rainstorm might be dramatic, but the picture will not be worth the risk.

If you get caught in the rain, protect the camera and dry it off as soon as possible. If you have access to a hair dryer, use it to dry the camera thoroughly. The newer model cameras with electronic features are especially susceptible to death by water. Use caution also with extended exposure to high humidity or a thick fog.

In an extremely humid (60 percent or more) environment, store your camera in a sealed container with silica when it's not in use. If you are planning a lengthy field season in a harsh climate, see the Bibliography.

When a Good Meter Goes Bad

If your light meter completely shuts down when the battery gets weak, you are lucky. Some systems continue to work with a weak battery and will give you incorrect meter readings for a long time before they quit. If your pictures turn out consistently light or dark, your battery and metering system should be checked out.

When you are suspicious of your meter reading, compare it with another camera set at the same film speed. If a second camera is not available, try the "sunny sixteen" rule: Set the f-stop at f/16 and meter a gray card or another medium tone that is in bright sunlight. (I used a red car bumper once—it worked.) If the meter is working properly, it will recommend a shutter speed that is equal to your film speed.

With Kodachrome 64 at f/16 in bright sunlight, the meter should recommend a shutter speed of a 60th of a second. There is a serious problem if it says to use a 15th of a second for this exposure. With no other battery and no other camera, check the battery connection by cleaning the interior contacts and both sides of the battery with a pencil eraser; or recalibrate the meter by adjusting the film speed until, in bright sunshine, you get a reading of f/16 at a 60th.

Coping with Battery Failure

When we consider all the things that could go wrong with the camera, battery failure is the most common problem. There is no cheaper insurance than routine replacement of the camera battery. Drop a spare in your camera case, especially before setting out for the hinterlands.

Newer cameras have many electronic features that exhaust batteries rapidly. I always start with a fresh battery. After a month in the field, a large collection of artifacts, and thirty rolls of film, however, it is going to quit.

If the battery failed completely, I could still use the "sunny sixteen" rule for an average exposure in sunlight. If I want to use a 200mm lens and a faster shutter speed, there are always reciprocal settings:

- f/16 at a 60th

- f/11 at a 125th

- f/8 at a 250th (with a telephoto in bright sun)

If my subject is in a shadow, I would add more light by using the next lower f-stop or the next slowest shutter speed. In dark shadow or heavy overcast, I may make a two-stop adjustment. I would also back up these guesses with several exposures, making sure that one will be good.

DARKROOM IN THE FIELD

With a little knowledge and a little equipment when developing black-and-white film in the field, you can do a lot of damage to the data you have collected. A darkroom technician will confirm that although the mechanics of producing an image on film are simple, success is also dependent on being familiar with the equipment; using consistent technique (which is only developed with experience); maintaining a draft-free, dust-free environment in which to dry film; having access to lots of clean, 68°F water; and packing all the necessary equipment and chemicals for processing and printing. If you must develop your pictures in the field, hire a darkroom technician or take along a Polaroid.

Even though field processing is sometimes advised as a useful check on equipment function, here are some more practical approaches to making sure that your equipment is in proper order:

- A preseason equipment check by a professional and routine field maintenance will reduce the chance of failure.

- If you are in a remote location for four months and your camera starts sounding a little funny after two, take a few test shots on a short roll of film and have it processed locally.

- If you do not have access to a local processor and you can't get your equipment repaired or replaced, start paying the illustrators to work overtime.

- When you have the only camera on the site and failure is out of the question, pack an extra camera body. It sounds troublesome, but it's a good alternative to coming back from two months of fieldwork with a week's worth of pictures.

AFTER THE SEASON ENDS

The essential tasks after the fieldwork is finished are choosing a good film processor, assembling your records carefully and thoroughly, and storing the processed film safely.

Choosing a Film Processor

After all that goes into taking good pictures, do not leave your film with just any lab that happens to be open the day you return home. When damaged, 35mm film is difficult to repair. A scratch may look like a phone line across your site. If dust was on the emulsion when it dried, you will have black spots on your slide or white spots on your print. Both are symptoms of sloppy handling and are almost guaranteed with any one-hour processing. For a small difference in price, there is often a large difference in the quality of processing.

To find a good professional lab, call a few independent photographers and ask where they have their processing done. I also recommend using Kodak's Colorwatch licensees. A camera store will usually have Colorwatch processing, and some drugstores or supermarkets may offer it. The quality is good and consistent. Or use the Kodak mailers (but don't mail your film to Texas in the summertime).

If you have experienced a ten-day wait to get Kodachrome processed, try to find a camera store or lab that uses the Kodak courier service, which provides a twenty-four– or forty-eight–hour turnaround on processing. If it's not available where you live, consider how old these artifacts are and try to keep the ten days in perspective.

Kodak's Ektagraphic HC is a high-contrast reversing film for white-on-black graphics. The first time I used this film, I just assumed that someone would be willing to process it. Kodak didn't want it nor did my professional lab. After making inquiries all over Denver, I finally found the Rocky Mountain Photo Lab. With any luck at all, you should be able to locate an independent processor who will give special handling to a single roll of film and work with you to get the results you need.

Maintaining Records

When the film is returned from the processor, force yourself to complete these last important tasks before shuffling and viewing:

- Put the rolls in chronological order.

- Compare the frame number on the slides or negatives to the frame numbers recorded in the log.

- Adjust the numbers in the log if necessary.

- Put the roll number and identifying data on each slide and print.

To record this information, use archival quality, fine-point pens available at art supply stores. It is also a good time to make notes on successes and failures. Put these notes in your camera case so that you are sure to review them before your next field season. As you view your photographs, edit out the bad ones—they will never get any better.

Storing Processed Film

Give some thought to elements that will destroy your processed film. Storing slides in their little yellow boxes or a drawer file subjects them to fingerprints, scratches, and dust when shuffled. The paper, glue, and plastics used in various boxes will eventually react with film. These same problems exist when negatives are left unprotected in the processor's envelopes. Notebook pages of polyethylene, polypropylene, or Mylar (usually labeled "archival") are available at many camera stores. These clear pages contain slots for each negative strip or slide. They provide a convenient space to identify a roll of negatives or a group of slides. You can view and select the ones you need without disturbing the rest. (Avoid any pages containing PVC or vinyl and glassine envelopes.) For a large project, a mail-order supplier may be the least-expensive source. See appendix C.

Some people believe that once the film is in such a page, it becomes indestructible—not so. Don't, for example, store them beneath the books on your desk. Here are some storage practices to minimize deterioration:

- Keep slides or negatives in those protective pages.

- Store pages in a binder to protect from scratches, punctures, spilled coffee, and light.

- Store notebooks in a metal cabinet (wood fumes can cause problems).

- Keep the temperature under 70°F.

- Maintain humidity at 40 percent or less.

(Agfa films have the reputation of being particularly vulnerable to high humidity [ASMP 1984].) These precepts are not difficult to follow. In a humid environment, it would be worthwhile to include a desiccant, such as silica gel, in the storage cabinet.

As they are used, slides may receive only about 90 percent dark storage under the best of circumstances. All by itself, this puts a dent in life expectancy. Daylight, light tables, projection, and heat will all take their toll. For example, fading will become noticeable after you have projected a slide for more than a half hour (thirty one-minute presentations), and deterioration is compounded if the slide is left on a light table, on a desk under fluorescent lighting, in sunlight, or locked up in a hot automobile. Get those irreplaceable shots duplicated and keep the original with the project record.

You can get an archival-quality print with black and white, but the process is expensive. The negative deserves the most attention—other prints can always be made. Of course, if negatives disappear, the print takes on new meaning. At the very least, prints should be stored individually in polyethylene or acid-free envelopes. You might also consider copying them (see chapter 6) and producing a negative in this manner or have them copied by a professional.

Chapter Six

In the Field

*I*n this chapter, we will walk through many field situations looking at various photo opportunities. We define goals and work out different strategies to meet each. Fortunately, conditions will not always be as bad as our examples suggest. Emphasis is placed on circumstances in which a casual approach can fail or where an alternative may improve results dramatically.

SITE FEATURES DEFINED BY LIGHT

The material used to construct a group of shelters, walls, mounds, or other features of a site is often a uniform-colored stone or adobe. This monotone can make it difficult to discern where one feature ends and another begins. By waiting for the sun to add just enough shadow to define and separate elements of the building, you can get an outstanding three-dimensional image. A slight shadow beneath the overhang of a roof makes the distinct visual impression that it extends toward the viewer. A small shadow caught at the top or side of a doorway will convey depth (see figs. 6.1, 6.2).

One of the more challenging sites I have photographed was a 180-acre site completely covered with an almost-white, round river stone. Mounds and partial walls attest to multicultural occupation as various techniques were employed to reuse this stone. However, an overall view taken at high noon looks like a river bottom. In the more oblique morning or afternoon light, there is enough shadow to define and give dimension to these elements.

The best light is the light that suits your subject. I was asked to photograph a stairway that was part of the Inka Road. It received a full shot of sunlight in the morning and was in shade in the afternoon. In both instances, the uniform light made it difficult to recognize dimension. By returning to the feature at high noon, I caught just a little bit of shadow, which effectively conveyed depth, as well as revealing elements of the construction.

If, for example, the subject consists of only two concourses of adobe brick, photographing it when a little shadow lends clear definition may be best. If you are lucky, you can take a break, eat lunch, and then the sun will be in a perfect position. If you are almost lucky, you will be coming back here tomorrow and can time your return for better light. Just in case, take this less-than-ideal picture anyway. One can never be too sure about tomorrow.

Figure 6.1 The structures of this Inca Period site are well defined by the late afternoon shadows.

Figure 6.2 With the sun directly overhead, a minimum amount of shadow identifies the rise in each step, giving this feature a readily discernible depth.

Perspective

Distorted perspective is a common problem when photographing architecture. This problem is evident as the sides of a building angle toward each other with height. Using a wide-angle lens can aggravate the problem. However, if your structure is surrounded by woods, a wide-angle lens may be your only choice for a comprehensive photo. To lessen or eliminate this distortion (fig. 6.3), you must match the plane of the camera to the plane of the subject, squaring up the camera for a straight-on shot (see chapter 1). To gain altitude, try standing in the bed of a truck or climbing a tree; the angle may let you show the entire structure in a natural perspective.

Keeping this type of vertical line away from the edges of the photograph will also help to reduce distortion. You may be able to back up, reduce the size of the image, and keep it in the center of the frame. Or, try shifting the camera down to bring more of the foreground into

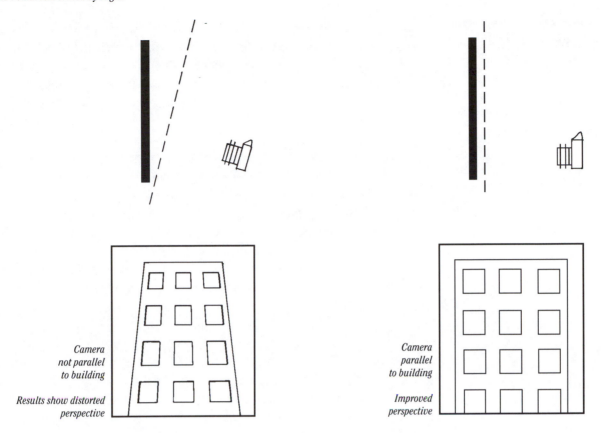

Camera
not parallel
to building

Results show distorted
perspective

Camera
parallel
to building

Improved
perspective

the picture and to better match the plane of the camera to the structure.

Figure 6.3 Perspective.

Standing alongside a low adobe wall (twenty inches tall, for example) to take its photograph may appear to reduce its dimensions. By getting the camera down to about ten inches off the ground, you will capture a more natural wall-like perspective.

If your project demands a lot of architectural photography and maintaining good perspective is therefore vital, you may be able to adapt a bellows system or a *perspective control* (PC) lens to your camera. Either will diminish distortion. They are, however, expensive and the bellows are bulky to pack.

Context

Photographing a complex site from a neighboring hillside will record a comprehensive view but will capture little detail. After taking the overall view, use a telephoto lens to break up the view into overlapping detailed enlargements. Because the photos have a common perspective, they are more useful in showing how a particular room relates to the site as a whole.

If there is no way to gain the altitude necessary for a comprehensive view, try for a perspective that can be easily related to a site plan. For instance, you might stand on the south side of a site, facing north, and take a comprehensive view of structures along this border. When you explain this site to others, the next photograph could be a site plan that demonstrates the relationship of the southern structures to the site as a whole.

Working with a site plan or detailed sketch can be very helpful—especially when the structures are numerous or complex. As photographs are

Orienting the Viewer: If you have
discovered an interesting feature at the
center of a complex site, orient your viewer to
its position with a site plan that highlights the
structure under consideration. Follow this
with photographs of the feature itself.

taken, you can easily note specific rooms, walls, features, and the direction
you are facing on the map, along with the frame numbers of the photographs.

A site study makes a valuable record of the project, and it also gets you
thinking about peripheral shots that show context and that seldom get
taken. As you leave the site, for example, pause a few times to take
(gradually) more comprehensive views. Be sure to note the name of the road
or trail you are on, any other identifiable landmark in these scenes, and the
direction you are facing as each is taken. Your route away from the site may
put you at an elevation that will afford a detailed view of the site with a
telephoto lens. Keep looking over your shoulder for possibilities.

A landscape photograph taken in bright sun will record different information than one taken under an overcast sky. A remarkable difference will also
be seen between morning and afternoon light. Taking a scene under a variety
of conditions can only add information to the record. In suitable light, a
polarizing filter can help to cut through glare and improve landscapes. (See
"Polarizing" below.)

Metering

Do not include the sky or the surrounding landscape in your meter reading.
Walk right up to the structure if necessary, get a reading only from this
subject, and then return to recreate your view. To show the light tone of
structures that have been whitewashed or are built of a very light-colored
stone, take the picture as metered, but follow up with one or two slightly
longer exposures that gradually add light. A dark subject should be gradually underexposed in this same manner (see chapter 2).

Don't limit yourself by trying to take one great picture of everything—no
one gets the perfect exposure every time. Have the patience to look for a
better angle or retake the photo in a different light. Keep in mind all the effort
that has gone into getting you this far. Investing a few extra frames of film to
get a good exposure is worth it.

Polarizing

If your subject is bathed in bright sunlight, try using a polarizing filter to cut
through the glare to reduce contrast and improve color. Replace any
ultraviolet (UV) or skylight filter on your lens with the polarizing filter. Tilt
the camera up (not left or right) for a view of the sky, then turn the filter until
the blue sky darkens and any white clouds are at their most distinct. Bring
the camera back down to the subject and take the meter reading with the
filter in this position.

The polarizing effect may be minimal if the sun is directly overhead or
behind you. If you cannot see the sky turn dark or other reflections being
eliminated from the subject, the filter should not be used.

Structural Detail

When you move closer to photograph just a portion of a wall you lose
context. Notes and a sketch should clearly relate that this view is, for
example, the exterior foundation at the center of the northwest wall (fig. 6.4).
Sketches need not be elaborate, just very clear. Add a scale when
possible, or include measurements in your notes. A photograph that
doesn't provide any clue to its context needs special handling when being

labeled. Without the specific details of what it is and where it was taken, most of its value is lost.

If an interesting detail is located in both sunlight and dark shadow, try to reduce the contrast. Have an assistant shade the entire view or hold a reflector to bounce some light into the shadows. On a shady side of the structure, lighten dark shadows with a strobe. Using a strobe in this manner can be informative, but the results may be unreliable. Don't use this method exclusively unless you are experienced with this fill technique.

To illuminate an artifact such as a grinding stone or adobe brick bearing a possible maker's mark, use a directional light, one that skims the surface and defines impressions. Ideally, the sky will be overcast and the artifact will lean at an angle producing soft shadows to lend clear definition. If a grinding stone is situated in bright sunlight, you might capture its dimension by shading the entire view. Then position a reflector in the sunlight to one side of the stone. Also consider the position of the camera. Holding the camera to your eye, move around the artifact to find a revealing perspective. It is surprising how often we have to lie down in the dirt for science. Don't forget notes, measurements, scale, and sketch.

When an object such as this adobe or grinding stone has captured your attention, follow up by recording its context. A wide-angle lens should afford the depth necessary to show the artifact in the foreground and other parts of the site behind it. The most important part of this scene is going to be the artifact; so, make sure the meter reading is just from this subject. Use a gray card, or one of the emergency gray cards, for metering. Be sure to bracket your exposure. A polarizing filter may be helpful, too.

EXCAVATION

Because an excavation is a process, you can get a visual record that is both informative and interesting if you are attuned to stages of development (beginning, middle, end). Take the time to photograph an artifact as it is being excavated, lifted out, and cleaned and, finally, its portrait. You will have a good record of context and technique, and a sequence that will involve the viewer in the discovery. Become alert to anything that suggests *process* and try to tell the story visually.

Preexcavation

When grid corners have been staked or flagged, preexcavation photography should cover the surface of the grid. Include a signboard showing the site or project name, grid coordinates, date, and an arrow (with a scale marked in centimeters) pointing north.

If more than one grid is to be excavated, a broad view of all should be taken. Your notes should include the direction you are facing. A simple sketch in your photo journal will identify each grid by its coordinates. If you have a telephoto lens, this first overview can be followed by an individual shot of each grid. By maintaining this perspective, you can relate each grid to the whole.

Mark the place you stand to take this photograph because it is helpful to recreate this same perspective as excavating proceeds. If a grid is to be extended, the setting of the pins should remind you to return to this spot to photograph the progress.

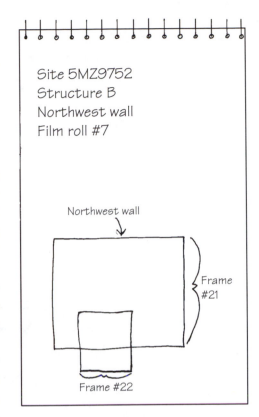

Figure 6.4 Notebook page and sketch.

Try to take a journalist's approach. Tell the story of what has brought you to this point. If nearby ruins or a distinctive geological feature contributed to the decision to excavate at this spot, attempt to show this relationship visually (fig. 6.5).

Work in Progress

Excavations do not proceed under picture-perfect conditions. However, photographs of an ongoing excavation should be made picture perfect. Although it is time-consuming, make sure that all equipment is moved aside, lines are set taut, loose dirt and trash are removed, and footprints are swept out. Make the signboard neat and legible; you should be able to read it as you look at it through the lens. The camera should be centered and level so that the horizon, floor, and walls are symmetrical. Nothing in the grid should conceal or distort any element. Don't distract the viewer with a red dustpan or bottle of suntan lotion. Don't convey a less-than-professional image by leaving a candy wrapper in the corner. Anything that indicates sloppiness will be noticed.

It is difficult to stand beside a hole in the ground and get a picture of everything in it. Our perspective cuts out the area adjacent to where we are standing, or the lens may not be wide enough to take in the whole grid. These problems are compounded as a grid increases in size and depth. Gaining altitude helps. You can place a camera over a grid by constructing a bipod (Harp 1975; Dorrell 1989) or a scaffolding to hold equipment and/or photographer. Remote triggering devices are discussed in chapter 4. Without such resources, another means to elevate the camera is needed.

Someone was once kind enough to carry a three-foot stepladder up the side of a mountain for me to use. Even from this lofty position, next to a grid of about one and a half meters, I still needed a 40mm wide-angle lens to cover the entire grid. (A 28mm-to-50mm zoom is a great lens to accommodate the constraints of a grid because of its flexibility.) The stepladder/wide-angle perspective was excellent. If you have only a 50mm lens, you may need to resort to overlapping photographs.

Any means at hand to gain altitude will help with perspective. You could back in a pickup truck, construct a ladder, or stand on a log or box. Whatever method is used, note the specifics so that the scene can be recreated if necessary. It may prove to be the best angle for a continuing series.

Without this elevated height (and distance), more consideration will have to be given to depth of field. Don't just focus on the signboard along the far wall or most of your depth of field will be wasted (see chapter 1, "Depth of Field"). Your view may extend from four feet in the foreground to eight feet at the most distant point on the floor. Check the depth-of-field guide on the lens to make sure that everything at these distances will be sharp.

Modifying Light

Count on the light being ugly and remember that shadows are detail-obliterating contrast. Without any means of reducing contrast, take one picture exposed for the light and one exposed for the shadow to make sure

a   *b*

that all details are captured. If you have a few assistants, you could try these methods to modify contrast:

- Hold a tarp so that the entire grid is shaded. It may sound dreary, but the results can be excellent.

- Use a piece of white cardboard, a space blanket that has been stretched very taut, or a sheet to reflect light into the shadows.

- Use a strobe on a remote cord, held so that it fills the shadows. Until you have some experience with what to expect from your strobe under these conditions, this method should be used only as a backup.

Using the same perspective and light from day to day makes it easier to follow the progress of an excavation, a consistency that will aid later analysis. If the sun is usually intense, the method of shading the entire grid will probably be the most reliable.

Emerging Feature

When your curiosity is aroused, you are looking at a part of the research process. Grab the camera and try to capture that intriguing element (fig. 6.6).

As a feature emerges from a floor, you need not wait to identify it before taking that first picture. If it turns out to be just another rock, you haven't lost much. As it projects above the floor, dimension may be shown best from a very low angle. Hold the camera to your eye as you move to find a good angle. Give it a good dusting with a brush, include a scale, shade to reduce contrast, or use a card reflector to fill shadows. If the subject warrants a second or third photo, try to duplicate the previous angle and light. If the feature turns out to be significant, back up a bit for a broader view, one that places it in the context of the grid. A signboard should be included at this point, as well as a stadia rod to document level. If the feature is not apparent in this overall view, fold a piece of notebook paper to form a neat arrow pointing to it.

When you want a photograph of an archaeologist working with a brush to uncover a feature, get right down there or use a telephoto. Fill the frame with a face, arm, brush, and feature. This is not the time to get another general view of someone wearing a red hat in a grid. Get a close shot, then get a closer shot.

Figure 6.5 At the Moche site of Huaca Rajada, this feature is known as the "Priest's tomb," an excavation that is approximately twenty feet deep. For the first view (a), I used a wide-angle lens, a small aperture, and lengthy exposure to capture sharp detail from the foreground surface to the floor of the tomb. The camera was focused at a point one third of the way into the scene, at a distance of about seven feet. If I had focused only on the floor of the tomb, the foreground and most of the wall detail would be blurred. In the second view (b), I changed to a telephoto and captured informative detail in a series that propels the viewer into the scene.

a

Figure 6.6 This ritually interred llama was excavated on the south coast of Peru. A more comprehensive view of the grid (a) places this feature (b) in context. The animal had been butchered, then all of the bones were wrapped in its skin and tied for burial. The in situ view was especially important because the relationship of these disarticulated bones shifted as they were excavated.

b

Wall Profiles

Wall profile photographs are mainly an aid to the completion of (more revealing) illustrations and to prove their accuracy (fig. 6.7). Good house-keeping includes brushing away loose dirt from wall and floor, moving buckets and tools out of the view, and setting lines taut. The signboard should note that this is, for example, the east wall. It should also include grid coordinates, the level of the excavation, the date, and an arrow pointing north.

A photograph of a profile will occasionally show a cut through a compacted floor or hearth, but such marked variation is rare. More often, we see only a smooth wall of uniform color. Even a notable change in soil texture is difficult to spot unless it also includes a change in color. To emphasize any variation in soil, use a spray bottle to mist the wall with water to bring out any color change or brush identifiable layers in opposite directions (vertical/horizontal/vertical) to vary reflected light.

If you take a close-up view of a particular element, be sure to pinpoint its position on the wall—or its value will be lost:

- Excavation levels can be marked by putting level numbers on a nail stuck into the wall. If you first photograph a wall that has been labeled in this way and then include one of these tags in your close-up, its context is preserved.

- If an element in the wall has been recorded as a distinct feature, you might make a simple paper arrow boldly lettered with the feature number. This arrow can be nailed to the wall or hung from a string to point to the feature. Take a first photograph of the entire wall with the arrow in place, and then take a close-up of the feature with the tip of the arrow showing.

Once again, direct sunlight can be a problem. Highlights and shadows are not as evident, but this contrast is splattered across the wall. To record the detail in each, either bracket the exposure or reduce contrast by shading the entire wall or by reflecting light into the shadows.

Figure 6.7 For this photograph of the wall profile of this one-by-one grid, the camera was set on a tripod as close to ground level as possible. This angle brings the camera almost parallel to the wall to minimize distortion and nearly replicates the view that will be shown in an illustration. The overcast sky helped modify the contrast between highlight and shadow. The distance that this view covers, from the foreground at the right of the frame to the horizon several feet behind the grid, is about six feet. To make sure everything is in sharp focus, I used a small f-stop for a lengthy exposure, and I focused at a point just in front of the signboard. The depth-of-field guide on the lens assured me that the depth extends from one to seven feet.

Standing and looking down at a wall causes the same type of distorted view as was discussed earlier. To keep corners straight and improve perspective, we must get the plane of the film to parallel the plane of the wall as much as possible, which usually means positioning the camera close to ground level.

From this ground-level angle, adjacent walls and floor fill the foreground. Depth of field becomes important (see chapter 1, "Stratigraphic Profiles"). To keep it all in focus, we'll need to use f/16, slow shutter speeds, and a tripod. If it is in the picture, we want it to be sharp. Without a wide-angle lens, the most detail will be recorded in two overlapping views with a 50mm lens.

A stadia rod upright in one corner presents a strong vertical line at the edge of the picture; it will emphasize any distortion in perspective. Place it toward the center of the picture if you can do so without hiding any important element in the wall.

ARTIFACTS

A photograph of any artifact will be at its most revealing if the subject is in a subdued light, a light that limits the intensity of both highlights and shadows. In the field, we use available daylight or a strobe to meet this goal:

- Use subtle highlights and shadows to reveal form, yet intentionally limit the degree of contrast between the two.

- Reduce the degree of contrast to work within the latitude of the film, ensuring that details are not lost in areas that are too bright or too dark.

In Daylight

One of the best times to photograph a three-dimensional object is when the sky is overcast. Little glare will reflect off a shiny surface, and harsh shadows are at a minimum.

On a sunny day, "bright shade" works best. Set up in a shady corner next to a white wall. The moderate light directed from both the sky and the wall enhances form, yet minimizes shadows.

When using either an overcast sky or shade for lighting, add a bit of light to any shadow that looks darker than necessary. Use a reflector when light seems to have little direction. Placing a white card so that light is bounced into a shadow can be a good way to make sure that every detail is discernible.

With a Flash

Taking a picture of an artifact with a flash or strobe is not my first choice, because you can't see exactly how the subject will be lit. Nonetheless, it is a practice I have had to resort to with every field trip. When you are forced to work indoors, having a *tested* method of taking a close-up with a strobe can mean the difference between success and failure.

A medium-power strobe and remote cord lets you place the light where it will provide the best coverage. Remove the flash from the camera so that no glare will bounce off the front of the artifact. A fairly powerful flash is helpful, but the amount of light that different units put out at close distances will vary. With lots of light, you can use very high f-numbers for good depth of field. With a single strobe held two to three feet from the subject, you can often use an aperture of f/16.

The blast of light should be as diffuse as possible. If the unit offers a setting for wide-angle coverage or a diffuser that can be placed over the light, use them. A layer of tissue paper will also help. Place a white card on the side of the subject away from the light so that a little light will reflect into shadows.

You can use a "soft box" attachment that fits over a strobe, which filters the light through white fabric. It does, however, reduce light intensity to the point that you may have to use a much less acceptable f/8 for a good exposure.

See chapter 4 for information about types of flash-metering systems. Your camera's manual will also be of help. It is important to test any strobe method before relying on it in the field:

1. The distance scale on the meter will indicate whether you can use f/16 at a distance of $2^1/_2$ feet or so.

2. Try a variety of placements, distances, diffusers, and backgrounds.

3. If your metering is through the lens, is the camera fooled by a black background? If so, and the artifact turns out overexposed, can you override the system and underexpose by a stop? Black works well to hide those nasty shadows, but if it causes overexposure, you may need a more neutral-colored background when using a flash.

4. If your camera and strobe synchronize at a 250th of a second, you can hand-hold the camera (but focus carefully). If they synchronize at a 60th of a second, you will be risking a blurred image with a hand-held close-up. Try it hand-held, then try the same picture with the camera on a tripod—the difference in sharpness will probably be worth it.

5. Test your technique. As long as you are carrying a flash unit, it is a little silly not to know what you can do with it.

Notes about how you achieved the best results should be kept with the unit to remind you of placement and settings.

With Multiple Flashes

A few years ago I was offered a slot on an expedition to Borneo *if* I could photograph orchids in the jungle trees. The challenges included:

- Dim light

- No tripod

- Getting maximum depth of field

- Minimizing shadows

My strobe and camera synchronize at a 250th of a second. With care, I can hand-hold a close-up at this speed. What I needed was a flash system to give me intense light so that I could use high f-stops for a maximum depth of field. The system also had to be flexible to achieve a minimum amount of shadow on a variety of subjects. I first tried a *ring light*, a flash unit that fits around the end of a lens and lights a close-up subject from all directions, but I was disappointed with the effects of this directionless light. And, having to get the light very close to the subject limited me to a 50mm lens. (I wasn't too thrilled with the price tag either.)

Figure 6.8 Camera and bracket.

I eventually found the simple bracket in figure 6.8. The camera attaches to the center, and a strobe can be placed on either arm. That's the way it is designed to be used, but I have yet to exhaust all the possibilities. This arrangement lets me use two flash units within inches of my subject, and I have enough light to use f/22 for depth. It also breaks down to three lightweight rods for packing.

You can also set up a useful field studio using this bracket on a tripod with a powerful main strobe at the center (instead of the camera). Two weaker strobes are placed on either arm. The weak strobes connect to the main unit, which connects to the camera with a remote cord.

You can place artifacts on a table next to this tripod light stand. The height and angle of the lights can be adjusted easily, and the camera is hand-held in the best position. When focusing is this critical, prefocus the scene, then fine tune the exact placement by moving the camera rather than turning the focusing ring. This arrangement gives you two steady hands on the camera, a big help even at a 250th of a second.

If your camera synchronizes with flash at a 60th of a second (instead of a 250th), you run a big risk of blurring the photograph in this close-up situation. If you need to use this setup, put the camera on a tripod.

Any strobe lighting system should be considered second choice to the reliability of working outdoors. Most lithic artifacts, bone, or glazed or polished surfaces will reflect so much glare that it is a waste of time to try to photograph them with a flash. And, the more accessories you rely on, the more can go wrong. Any time success depends on AA batteries, you are living on the edge. Other hazards include equipment failure, incorrect settings on the strobe or camera, and reflected glare.

Even with all the risk, having such a tested alternative at hand has meant being able to get hundreds of photos that would otherwise not have been taken. All three flash units and the bracket are lightweight and small enough to fit in my tripod case for travel. The bracket is available by mail, or you could make your own (see Shaw 1987). A large photo supply store may have another alternative.

ACCESSORIES TO THE SCENE

Accessories need to be considered in two ways: those things that add to the information we record, and those things that distract from or distort the subject. To add information, we place the artifact in its most revealing perspective and include a legible scale and catalog number.

Backgrounds

The background should have zero impact—no texture, shadows, marks, lint, or anything that causes the eye (and mind) to wander from the subject. Black velvet (about a yard and a half is best) may seem an exotic accessory, but it is surprisingly durable and one of the easiest backgrounds to work with. It resists reflecting light better than black felt, construction paper, or flat black paint. The uniform shadowless background dramatically sets off most any subject. (An added advantage is that black facilitates an informative double-exposure.) To take care of your velvet, you'll need a wad of masking tape to pick up lint and a line to hang it on when you need to get rid of wrinkles. Use a slightly damp cloth to brush off any dirt and to speed up the process of getting wrinkles out.

Plain white is my second choice for backgrounds. It is particularly useful when the subject is very dark or when using black-and-white film. Rather than pack a white background, I usually wait until the illustrators have gone to lunch. . . and then borrow one.

Avoid colored backgrounds because they can easily reflect their color onto the subject. You don't want to change the color of an artifact with a shift induced by a colored background or by placing it next to a colored wall.

Showing an artifact on a picnic table or concrete slab conveys a casual attitude toward handling artifacts and draws attention away from the subject. If this is your only possibility, find a spot on the slab that is as uniform as possible in color and texture. Or, you might also drag a clipboard through sand to level it, or sweep a smooth spot in dirt. If the edge of a backdrop or table is in the view, change to a longer lens (from a 50mm to an 80mm or 105mm).

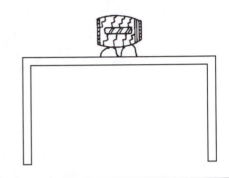

Figure 6.9 Vessel propped up.

Props

Getting an artifact into a position to show its form, technology, or a design element can call for a bit of creativity. Setting a vessel in its natural upright position may obscure information about the shape of its base. Similarly, if we stand an anthropomorphic figurine on its little anthropomorphic feet, we could spend a long time trying get the light to fill those detail-obscuring anthropomorphic shadows.

Several wads of Silly Putty can be placed under an artifact to hold it steady and in a position complemented by the light (fig. 6.9). Doing so also lifts it away from the background to minimize harsh shadows. Separating the subject from the background in this manner also helps to keep the background out of focus. Any imperfection on it should be blurred beyond recognition.

When I was photographing a collection of ceramic vessels at the Smithsonian, one of the conservators frowned at my plastic egg full of "oil-based plastic." She gave me a small beanbag to use instead. Although I have never noticed any residue remaining on an artifact, I pass along the observation. The beanbag worked, but it is sometimes more convenient to be able to stick an odd-shaped artifact firmly at a good working angle. Modeling clay also works if it is kept from drying out. Other useful props are small stones, match boxes, and film cans.

A roll of masking tape is another item I often reach for. It can lift little bits of junk off the background and keep fabric and scales tacked down.

Scales

A scale must be legibly numbered and positioned within the picture's depth of field for sharpness. I have yet to find a standard white ruler that does not include extraneous and distracting advertising. Clear plastic scratches easily and picks up reflections, as does silver. With the aid of a typewriter for a very small-scale scale, graphic tape for a distinct line on a large-scale scale, and a few rub-on numbers, I can manufacture a scale to suit most any need.

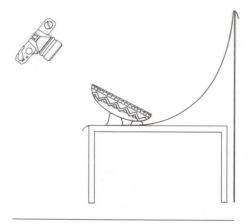

Figure 6.10 Bowl on table.

One scale I often use runs 20 cm in length. I use both a vertical and a horizontal version and have had it copied onto white card stock so that I can take along several of each. Scales have a way of getting misplaced, blown away, or bent, folded, and stained. (Some copiers will reduce the size of anything they copy; so, be sure to check for its accuracy.)

Trimmed to about four by eight inches, the scale can be held securely in place and at an appropriate height by inserting the blank edge between the pages of a book. The book will not be seen in the photograph; it is merely a simple device to keep the scale flat and at an easily adjusted height within the depth of field. The book is placed to one side of the artifact so that the printed scale extends as far into the scene as is necessary. If the plane of the scale does not match the artifact, prop up one end of the book to a appropriate angle. This method ensures that the scale remains in a useful relationship to the artifact and within the depth of field for sharpness.

For the artifact in figure 6.10, I would run a ruler-sized scale along the bottom of the picture. A wad of Silly Putty at each end holds it in place. Bowls are exceptionally difficult to photograph because they require a maximum amount of depth. Tilting at this angle allows the scale to be placed behind the front edge well within this depth, and there is good light on both interior and exterior surfaces.

Catalog Numbers

Catalog information must also be included. Use a felt-tipped pen to record data in legible black ink. Make sure to have a selection of broad, medium, and fine point pens to scale lettering to the subject. An erasing template can help keep lettering straight and of a uniform size. An index card works well because it is a good weight, and it can be cut to extend the data from just behind the scale, keeping it in the same plane as the scale and artifact. Once I had the luxury of using a typewriter. . .until the lab crew returned from lunch. My kit includes plain white index cards; broad, medium, and fine point felt-tipped pens; ruler or erasing template lettering guide; scissors; and tape. Don't forget to write the catalog numbers in your photo log. Include brief description of the artifact to help resolve any numbering errors.

TECHNIQUES WITH ARTIFACTS

Taking close-ups is probably the most demanding task in field photography:

- When the subject is close, depth of field is minimal. Consider the best angle for the subject and focus carefully to place that small area of sharpness where it is needed most.

- The slightest camera movement is exaggerated and will blur details; so, use a tripod.

- The artifact is often on a high-contrast background, one that can confuse the light meter. Keep a gray card handy and use it.

Getting a large detailed image is the object. Situate the camera and tripod to match the most important plane of the subject and get as close as possible.

a

b

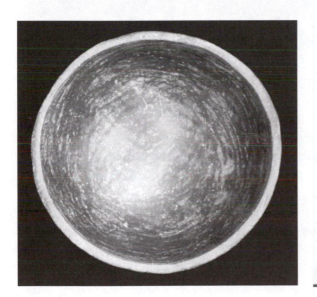

c

d

Empty space around an artifact contributes nothing and reduces the size of the image and the amount of detail. Check every lens you have to see which one will be your best close-up lens. Set each at its minimum focus and look at a ruler. The one taking in the fewest inches is your best magnification (fig. 6.11)

Figure 6.11 Studying a vessel. (a) Nice shot of an incised, footed bowl. Scale is legible, your notes state that red slip is uniform but slightly worn, wall is sixty millimeters thick, incising one to two millimeters deep, reveals gray paste, fine temper. Don't quit now. After the first pretty picture is taken, let's consider some of the other questions an analyst may ask. (b) Is the design element uniform? How many times is it repeated? How many feet are there? (c) Are there any design or diagnostic finishing marks on the rim or interior? (d) How tall is it?

Moistening Ceramic

If a ceramic is intact enough to have been washed, use a cotton ball to remoisten the sherd slightly to bring out the color of the paste and paint. Fugitive paint (a water-soluble paint that may be completely removed from the surface of the vessel but traces of which have been trapped in the pores of the paste) may also be revealed by moistening. (Be sure to dry the ceramic thoroughly before returning it to a plastic bag.)

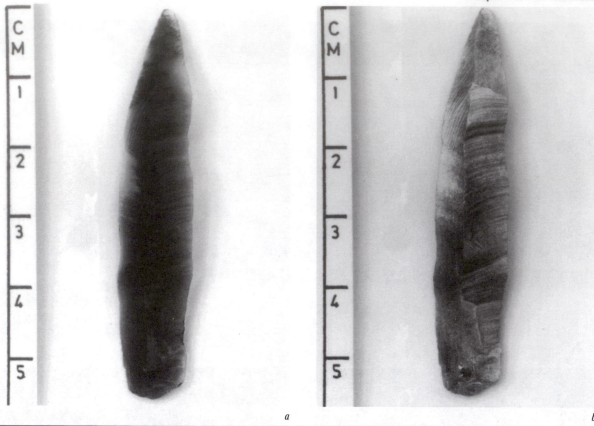

a   *b*

Figure 6.12 Blade with and without aluminum powder. This translucent blade (a) has few ridges to catch defining highlights. Also, the surface detail seems to be blurred by the image coming through the back of the blade. Altogether, this is a poor picture of an artifact. In the second view (b), the blade was photographed after being dusted with a light coat of aluminum powder. Some of the ripples along the upper surfaces are now apparent.

Lithics

My favorite flintknapper challenged me to come up with a field technique to photograph an assortment of lithic points, blades, and drills made from a wide variety of stone. His criticism of the results convinced me not only that flintknappers are hard to please but also that there is no one best method to use on such an artifact.

Where highlights are used to reveal shape, such as on an obsidian point, these highlights pose the ultimate contrast to the black material. Information at both extremes is lost. A point made from a metavolcanic coarse-grained stone will resist any such definition by light. Flake scars may lack distinctive ridges, and the material seems to absorb more light than it reflects. For a highly reflective surface, use a diffused light to lessen contrast. For a material that resists highlighting, use a much more intense light.

A simple and effective opaquing technique is to coat an artifact with aluminum powder (Callahan 1987). It is especially useful with translucent or black obsidian (fig. 6.12). Form becomes readily discernible as contrast is reduced. The powder does hide information about the type of stone and obscured diagnostic conchoidal ripple, retouch scars, and evidence of use-wear. A small vial of aluminum powder and a paintbrush can be useful to make a high-contrast or translucent surface opaque to show overall form and perhaps to compare form among several artifacts, but don't use it when you need to demonstrate technology or use.

A highly reflective yet colored material, such as jasper, can benefit from the use of a polarizing filter on the camera to reduce bright highlights. Because a translucent stone is dependent on light for definition, you may be left with a shapeless mass when you remove the highlights. When glare obscures rather than defines the artifact, a polarizing filter will be useful.

a   *b*

Distinctive ridges on the surface of translucent objects may be blurred by the out-of-focus image coming through from the reverse side. Methods for making the reverse side opaque (with a water-based paint or marker, or a mix of india ink and soap) are messy. By placing a translucent blade on black velvet in bright shade, you can get a sharp image of only the ridged surface. However, diagnostic information about the color of the rock may be lost if translucence is hidden. So, some lithic artifacts will not lend themselves to a single comprehensive photograph. If you take up the study of stone tools, you would do well to also master illustrating.

For a highly reflective stone, diffuse the source of light. Work in shade or diffuse direct light with a piece of frosted Mylar (available at art supply stores). Place reflectors to fill in details along the base or notches. With so many facets to gather reflections, be careful that the red pickup truck parked nearby does not become part of the picture.

A clipboard like the ones illustrated in figures 6.13 and 6.14 is useful for positioning less-reflective artifacts that are complemented by a very directional light. (Several coats of flat black paint and a wad of Silly Putty may be all you need to set up a point.) A book holder or other prop can position the board so that light will just graze the surface of the artifact. A scale can be included and held in this same plane with more Silly Putty. The bottom clip or masking tape will hold a reflector in place.

The cut marks on bone, a bone tool, or an incised or worked shell will often benefit from this type of directional light. Cut marks can be especially elusive unless they are carefully highlighted. Position the artifact and scale firmly on the board, then view it through the camera as you turn the board to find the best light. It may be necessary to have an assistant diffuse the light with a piece of tracing paper or frosted Mylar, or use a reflector to counter harsh shadows (fig. 6.15). Use a gray card for metering and bracket your exposure.

Figure 6.13 Taken with a one-second exposure at f/32 using a macro lens, this obsidian point (a) rests on a piece of putty, which holds it steady and up from the background. Shadows are softened and minor imperfections in the background are obscured. The second view (b) shows how the artifact was set up. The clipboard is tilted for better light and a reflecting card brings out the detail around the base of the point, even in the shade. A small book holds the scale and catalog number on a plane that is in sharp focus.

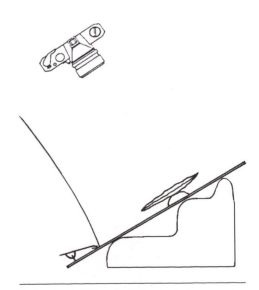

Figure 6.14 Clipboard, point, and reflector.

a

b

Figure 6.15 This assortment of three points has been set directly on the background. In the first view (a), the camera was hand-held at 125th of a second (too slow to get sharpness) with an aperture of f/11 (which reduced the depth of field). Bright sunlight produced increased contrast and confusing shadows. In the next view (b), a tripod was used with a one-second exposure at f/32. Shade was introduced to soften shadows and modify the degree of contrast between the light and dark surface detail. Very little detail is either too light or too dark for the film to record.

Points are most commonly positioned with the distal edge toward the top of the picture. The strongest light will be on the upper lateral margins. Examine published photos of points to learn about what needs to be accomplished. Recreating a particular example may depend on both the type of stone and the thickness of the cross section. When you try to bounce light around a thick point, you may discover that those little ridges take on the proportions of mountain valleys. Be patient.

Meter from a gray card and make sure to bracket your exposure. Depending on the type of stone and amount contrast, an overexposure or underexposure may be the best.

Double Exposure

To discover whether your camera allows you to double expose a picture, check your camera manual. A single picture showing both front and side views of a vessel is a good way to demonstrate form. You can show the front and back of a figurine, the top and side profiles of a spindle whorl, the handle and figure on a stamp (fig. 6.16), or the interior and exterior of a ceramic mold. I once made a triple exposure of an incised bone flute. The instrument was turned slightly in each exposure to follow the design element.

Because the subject is placed in each half of the frame, you must use a Fresnel viewing screen for focusing rather than a split-image screen. The style with a grid overlay helps to keep the subject centered in each half of the frame.

Once again, the best background is black velvet because when you make the first exposure, the film records just this image. No light comes from the other side of the picture, and so the film is unaffected. A colored background would be recorded on the film and fade the second image. So, start with a wrinkle-free, lint-free piece of black velvet and follow this procedure:

1. Place the first view in one half of the frame. The scale and artifact number can be alongside or run completely across the bottom of the frame.

2. Use a gray card to get the meter reading.

3. Carefully note the image size and placement within the half-frame so that the artifact can be placed in a similar position in the other half.

4. Take the first picture and have an assistant standing by to shout, "Don't advance the film." Cock the shutter according to your camera manual but don't advance the film.

5. For the second exposure, remove the scale and artifact number and place the new view of the artifact in the second half of the frame. Everything else in this view is black, and so the first image is not changed.

6. Camera settings for the second exposure will be the same as for the first.

Don't use a strobe for a double exposure—because even black velvet will reflect light with a double shot from a powerful flash. An overcast sky or bright shade is best. A subdued studio light should work well also.

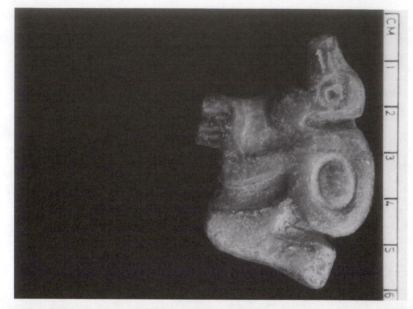

c

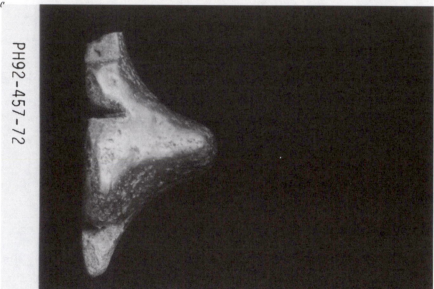

b

PH92-457-72

Figure 6.16 This type of ceramic stamp was used in Ecuadorian cultures to adorn bodies as well as textiles and ceramic vessels. To show in a single photograph the figure on the face of the stamp and the handle as it was used to impress the design, I made a double exposure. First I carefully cleaned the black velvet background, set up subdued light, and put the camera on a tripod. For the first exposure (a), the stamp is upright, and putty is wrapped around the handle to form a sturdy base. The scale is included in this view, the stamp is centered in the right half of the frame, and the left half is completely black. After taking the meter reading from a gray card, I take the picture and re-cock the shutter, but I do not advance the film. For the second exposure (b), the stamp is turned on its edge to show the design of the handle. Again, it is held in this position with a piece of putty beneath the handle. The catalog number is included, and the stamp is centered in the left half of the frame. After taking another meter reading from the gray card to ensure consistency, I take the picture. The final picture (c) shows the two views in a single frame.

c

COPYING DOCUMENTS

Copying a document, map, or other graphic can be accomplished in good order if a source of uniform light is available (fig. 6.17). An aperture of f/8 will produce the best resolution for a finely detailed image. In bright sunlight, this means you can hand-hold Kodachrome 64 or T-Max 100 at a speed of a 250th of a second. Be sure to use a gray card to determine the exposure; the setting will be very different from metering only the subject (see also chapter 2).

It is important to hold the camera in a position that is centered over and parallel to the document. The image will not be distorted by an odd angle, and the plane of the subject will be within the limited depth of field.

For copying many documents, use a tripod. A small level can be used to make sure that the back of the camera is parallel to the subject. (See chapter 7 for more tips and cautions on copying documents and on using a tripod as a copy stand.)

Using a Flash

If you expect to be photographing many documents or are working indoors, the bracket and dual-strobe setup mentioned earlier will be helpful. Each strobe can be positioned on either side of the camera at a 45° angle for a uniform light. This system can be efficient with a nonreflective subject, but be sure to test it *with* the particular film you intend to use. If the flash units are too close to the page, uneven light will mar the results. Because metering is done automatically, it may be necessary to set the camera to overexpose the picture so that a white document does not turn gray. Keep good notes on the arrangement that tested best so that it can be duplicated in the field.

Backlighting a Map

A map that uses color to show a variation in topography can be more revealing if it is hung in a sunny window for backlighting. The sun should be absolutely uniform (no shadows, no dirt on the window), and the map must be hung flat. If one corner is pulled a bit tighter than the rest, the stress on the paper will be recorded.

Place the camera so that it is centered and the film plane (back of the camera) is parallel to the map. We are not using reflected light in this situation; metering on a gray card is therefore useless. Meter the subject and then overexpose one half, one, and one and a half stops to ensure a good exposure. (I often find that overexposures turn out the best.)

For a large detailed map, the higher resolution of Kodachrome 25 can improve results—giving a sharper definition to the fine line in place names, roads, and topographic data.

INTERIORS

When you must photograph the interior of a room with a strobe on the camera, try for a view that does not include anything between you and the subject. The flash will overpower an item in the foreground and probably cause your subject to be underexposed. With a remote cord, you can use the strobe off the camera and direct light around such an intrusion.

a

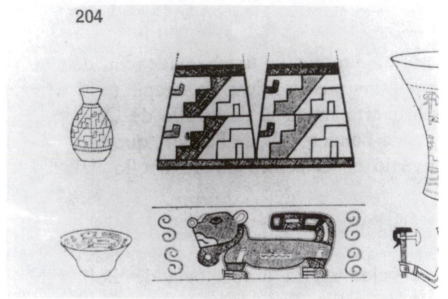

b

Figure 6.17 Copying an illustration from a book. In the first view (a), the subject is in bright sun, the page is held flat, and the camera is parallel to the page. With a flat subject and a bright light, I hand-held the camera at f/8. Two problems are apparent. First, the page is thin and text from the reverse is showing through. Second, because metering was taken from the subject and not a gray card, the meter (successfully) recommended an exposure to render the white page gray. To correct this problem, I inserted a black paper behind the page, which obscured the text from the reverse. Then I read the light from a gray card, rather than the white page, to set the exposure. In this view (b), white, black, and gray are all reproduced appropriately. The final view (c) is my insurance shot. Because some of the "black line" on this illustration is only a row of dots, I wanted to make sure that even these would be apparent. So, I darkened the illustration overall by underexposing by one full stop.

c

With a tripod and cable release, you may have enough light to calculate a lengthy exposure (see chapter 1, "Apertures and f-stops"). Be sure to bracket; underexposure is a common film failure with long exposures.

If the room includes a window with light coming through it, as well as a dim interior, allow for this high contrast. Remember that the film will not record good detail in both light and dark areas: Meter the most important subject, and bracket to include the whole range of tones. It may help to reduce contrast if you cover the outside of the window with white paper, use a reflector in a pool of light on the floor to bounce light into a dark area, or use a strobe aimed at just the dark area.

Museums

When the museum collection is important to your research, follow this procedure:

- Investigate. Along with hours and admission, find out the rules on cameras, tripods, and single-legged monopods.

- See chapter 3 for film choices.

- Depth of field will be minimal. Assess the artifact for its most informative angle. Then match the plane of the film (back of the camera) to the most revealing angle.

- Take good notes on the artifacts. Data on size and provenience are easy to forget.

Black Holes

Caves, dark basements, kivas, or other black holes usually call for a wide-angle lens, but the coverage is very uneven when such a large area is lighted with a single flash. Instead, set up the camera on the tripod, open the shutter, and use several well-placed flashes to fill in various parts of the picture gradually. The strobe is not attached to the camera in any way. The results are impossible to predict, but it is the sort of creative technique that makes you look forward to getting those pictures back. When it works, it works well.

This technique requires a tripod and cable release, an assistant *or* a cable release that will *lock* to keep the shutter open all by itself, and a strobe. Here's the procedure:

1. With the camera on the tripod, aim the camera at the scene (a flashlight is often helpful). Set the aperture to its smallest opening (f/16, for example). Set the shutter speed to B so that the shutter stays open for as long as the shutter button is pressed.

2. Consider what is in the scene and estimate the distance of the camera to the foreground and to the most distant point.

3. If the scene takes in from five to twenty feet, these distances must be set within the 16s on the depth-of-field guide on the lens. In this case, the camera will be focused at around ten feet. *Leave the focus set at this distance.*

4. The next step is to check out the strobe. Make sure that the ISO of the film has been set on the strobe; then read the recommended distance

to the subject for f/16. (For instance, with ISO 64 and f/16, a medium power strobe may need to be three feet from the subject, and a more powerful unit can be placed six feet away.)

5. Walk around the interior and estimate the best placement of flashes when the strobe is held at the distance your unit recommends. Floor or ceiling may also be lit. This may take only a couple of flashes, or it might take six or seven in a deep cave with many irregular niches to light.

6. Plan ways to hold the strobe so that you do not come between the light and the camera when the flash is set off.

7. Use the cable-release lock or have an assistant hold the cable-release plunger to open the shutter. It must stay open until all flashes have been completed. (When such a small aperture is used in a very dark setting, the shutter can stay open for a long time with little effect on the film.)

8. Go to those places you have decided to light and press the flash's test button. Hold your hand over any recharge indicator or dial light on the strobe, so that the camera does not pick up this light.

9. When the last flash is fired, close the shutter.

10. Try several exposures, varying the distance to the subject slightly, and increasing or decreasing the estimated overlap of light.

In a Hurry

Being given an opportunity to photograph an unusual artifact from a private collection can cause all our good technique to disappear. Try anything and bracket the exposure. This is not a time to save film. (See fig. 6.18.)

- Try to diffuse light as much as possible by shading the subject. If you must use direct sunlight, try to reduce contrast by reflecting light into dark shadows.

- Find a scale to include in the scene.

- Match the angle of the camera to the most revealing angle of the subject to use whatever depth of field is available.

- If you do not have a gray card, make certain that metering is not thrown off by a high-contrast background.

- After taking the first picture, get a second one that overexposes by a full stop, and a third that underexposes by a full stop. Bracketing will make sure that details in highlights and shadows are recorded.

- Reduce camera shake with deep, steady breathing, and wait to squeeze the shutter until the end of an exhale.

- Get complete notes on the location, owner, provenience, and dimensions.

- Make another note to keep a gray card and scales in your camera bag.

a

b

c

Figure 6.18 A no-frills studio uses simple accessories and basic technique to get a picture in a hurry. The first view (a) shows the setup: roll of tape, egg full of Silly Putty, gray card, construction paper taped down to surface, and vessel held in position with putty. The equipment is set in the shade or under an overcast sky so that the shadows are very soft. In the photographer's notebook, frame number, vessel dimensions, catalog number, location, and comments are recorded. In the second view (b), the front of the vessel is sharp, but the neck and edges are blurred. I hand-held the camera at a 60th of a second at f/5.6. You will get better results with a flat surface under these conditions. In the final view (c), the entire vessel is now reasonably sharp. I used an 8th of a second exposure at f/16 with the camera on a tripod. To use this increased depth of field, I focused on the front edge of the neck.

Figure 6.19 During a site survey in a Peruvian valley, our team was confronted with the site of an ancient cemetery that had been exposed by a break in a modern irrigation ditch. Viewing the overall damage, I used as much depth of field as I could muster to gather the foreground detail in a sense of the breadth of devastation as it continued up the ravine. The dislodged, mummified youth posed a shocking vision as he was found standing alongside this chaos. Because of constraints on the survey, nothing was collected or disturbed. The sunlight could not have been more intense. To make sure that this unhappy discovery was recorded, each exposure was carefully bracketed.

ON A SITE SURVEY

A site survey may involve a few hours or a month and, start to finish, there is a visual record to maintain. It can be helpful to have a copy of the field map to use with your photo log. On the map you can pinpoint exactly where pictures are taken and use an arrow to show the direction of a particular view.

Creating a Visual Map

Documenting your location and route is made easier if photographs include a peak or other distinguishing feature that is also on your map. Notes should identify this feature and the direction you are facing.

When you spot an interesting feature in the distance, take a moment to set the scene for others. Start with a wide-angle lens and note "Pike's Peak on the horizon at 2 o'clock, feature just left of center at 8 o'clock." Then, from this same perspective, use a standard lens centering on the feature. Then use a telephoto. A storytelling sequence lets the viewer experience the discovery. Maintaining this visual map also contributes environmental and geographical data to the record. It aids future researchers who must reconstruct your work, and it provides a context for those who view the results (fig. 6.19).

The Immovable Object

When you discover a cut mark in the side of a tree (or any other feature that can't be propped up in the best light with Silly Putty), try everything you can think of to get the picture. In a remote location, for example, I was confronted with a headstone that bore both scratched lettering and shallow incising. These were barely discernible in the full blast of morning light. I took the picture, then used a strobe to add a directional light across the incising. I hoped that a bit of shadow would give some indication of its depth. Later in the day, with the stone in full shade, I took the same photograph again. Each photo revealed different information. The direct light seemed to emphasize the scratches, the oblique light from the strobe showed the incising, and the shade produced the best information on the type of stone.

By trying to think of the one best way to take the picture you may limit the record needlessly. For an immovable object:

1. Work with the plane of the object and consider multiple angles.

2. Vary the light as much as possible by increasing or decreasing contrast (using reflectors, strobe, or creating shade).

3. Include a scale and make a sketch that notes dimensions.

4. Move in for close-up detail; back away for context.

5. Bracket the exposure.

6. If you have tried everything in your bag except the polarizer, try the polarizer.

When investigating an unusual feature that you may be asking others to interpret, do not risk hindering or misleading a specialist with incomplete or field-edited information.

Rock Art

A pictograph will vary in every instance, but we do have one constant: the opportunity to photograph it is limited. We can try one or two shots and hope they work out, or improve the odds by investing half a roll of film and some imagination:

1. Ideally, the light will be a *uniform* sun or shade. If part of a mural is in shade, try to cast shade on the rest. A strobe will probably add more light to shadows than a reflector, but its coverage is limited. If possible, try both.

2. If an image is faint, bracketing may capture it. Or, wait for the sun to move. Sun, shade, or strobe may bring out the design the best.

3. Black-and-white film used with a yellow filter may be useful to increase the contrast between a faint dark paint and light-colored rock.

4. Never emphasize a design with chalk or by any other means—it's called *vandalism*.

5. Paint that is in full sunlight will be muted by glare. Try a polarizing filter to cut through the reflection.

6. The color of paint may contrast dramatically with the rock. Use a gray card for meter reading.

7. Match the plane of the camera to the plane of the rock as much as possible.

8. Move in for detail and back away for context.

AERIAL PHOTOGRAPHY

Most references that combine the words "aerial" and "archaeology" begin by describing how to mount a cartographic camera in your plane because it is the best way to conduct remote sensing. Most projects, however, could not fund more than eleven minutes of flight time, much less the necessary camera or film. Making friends with a pilot is often the only option.

The results of hanging a 35mm camera out the window of a plane are inconsistent because the variables are almost unlimited. The quality of the photographs is affected by weather, haze, altitude, time of day, shutter speed, lens type, film type, metering, the contrast of site features, and seasonal changes in vegetation. Why bother? Because these photographs can reveal information. So, if you have made friends with a pilot, here are some tips:

- Load a fresh roll of film so that you don't have to try to reload while in the plane.

- Borrow a second camera and load it with another roll.

- Use Ektachrome 200 and T-Max 400 black-and-white film so that you can use fast shutter speeds. You must use a fast shutter speed to overcome the plane's vibration.

- A telephoto lens can give you the best definition of a site. You should not expect to produce a map; simply getting an overall view of the site may be the most realistic goal. The narrower angle of view of a telephoto will also be an advantage when you must shoot through the plane's struts. A lens in the 100mm to 200mm range should probably be your first choice.

- Vibration will cause zoom lenses to change focal lengths. You can also be distracted by trying to find the best magnification when all you should be thinking about is your subject. Opportunities come and go rapidly. Tape the zoom at its longest focal length and get on with taking pictures.

- Tape the focus at infinity so that it is not shifted by vibration.

- Set the f-stop to f/5.6 or f/8 for the best resolution. Depth of field will not be a factor.

- Absolute minimum shutter speed from a plane is a 250th. If metering allows a 500th at f/8, so much the better. (In a helicopter, a 500th of a second is a minimum.)

- The meter reading should be taken only from the ground, not the horizon. Including the sky in the meter reading will most likely cause underexposure.

- Both a lens shade and a UV or skylight filter should be used. With an ISO 400 black-and-white film you should have enough light to use a yellow filter instead of the UV. The film is fast enough to reduce light with a filter and still use an ideal f/8, a 500th of a second exposure. If you are using an ISO 100 black and white, don't use the yellow filter because it may reduce light to the point that you must use less-than-ideal settings.

- Don't even think about trying to fuss with a polarizer.

- If anyone gives you a choice of aircraft, make it a high-winged variety. Taking pictures through a wing is not currently possible.

- Plead for an open window to shoot through. A quarter-inch-wide acrylic "filter" tends to degrade results.

- Your body will cushion some of the plane's vibration by the time it works its way up to your hands; so, don't brace an arm or your camera on any part of the plane.

- The low-angle light of early morning or late afternoon will give a clear definition to a site on flat terrain. A mountain site may only stand out at 2 o'clock in the afternoon. The best time is going to be when some shadows are present to lend depth and definition to features.

- Air is usually less polluted in the morning. However, if the weather is normally foggy in the morning, don't sit and wait for the fog to lift, then go up in the flat light at noon. Plan a late afternoon flight instead.

- Ask the pilot to circle the site, varying both radius and altitude. As these change, along with the changing angle of the sun, your results will be remarkably different.

- If you must pause to change film or equipment, try to do so when you are between the sun and the site. The pictures that you miss, with the sun at your back and uniform light on your subject, will usually be the least revealing.

- If you have the opportunity to repeat this process, do it. A different time of day, a different season, or an unusual climate occurrence such as a drought will all provide different information.

- If you have experience with infrared film and understand the complex problems of handling and determining a good exposure, you may wish to try a roll in a third camera.

If you can take most of the steps outlined above, the photographs should be worthwhile. If you get interested in remote sensing, see the Bibliography for references on aerial photography.

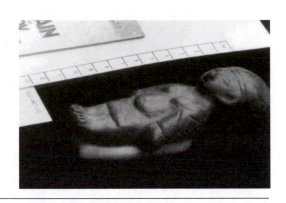

In the Studio

I was given the opportunity to sit in on one of Warren Blanc's studio sessions. To better introduce him and his approach to photography, I will describe some of what I saw. The walls and ceiling of the studio are painted flat white. A work table is across one end of the room. A long roll of white background paper is hung on the wall and pulled down in a curve to cover the table.

The client's art director and assistant have been working here for two days to perfect the layout of graphic supplies for an advertisement. About five feet above and to one side of this layout is a single tungsten-halogen lamp positioned so it bounces light off a curved piece of foamcore. As this softened light falls from the top and side, the layout is lit very subtly with a continuous gradation in tone and no bright highlights or dark shadows.

After a few Polaroids have been taken to refine composition, the four-by-five film is loaded. Even though the studio camera is mounted on a stand that would support a small building, everyone is instructed to be seated and hold still. The meter suggests f/64 for fifteen seconds. Watching the second hand on the clock, he takes five different exposures of this scene, at five, ten, fifteen, twenty, and twenty-five seconds. Experience does not teach you which exposure is best. Why on earth would he bracket the exposure this extensively for a scene he has shot a thousand times before? *Experience.* Experience reinforces the lesson that you don't know which exposure is best—but you had better get the picture or take up computer programming.

His studio is filled to the brim with expensive light banks and a myriad of background alternatives, but it's not the fancy equipment, it's the technique. Simplicity is what works. In this case, a single reflected light was appropriate to the subject—an approach well suited to artifacts. With this introduction to a studio, we'll turn to Warren for advice on how to get there from here.

ADVANTAGES OF THE STUDIO

After battling the wind, dirt, limited accessories, and unpredictable sunlight in the field, you'll find that being able to plug in and turn on a sun or two is a luxury. The controlled environment, reliable accessories, and the time—and patience—to take advantage of each are the means to producing a professional quality photograph of an artifact.

The single most telling attribute of this photograph is the absence of any glaring bright highlight or dark shadow. Harsh light looks unnatural and will conceal information about your subject. To reduce contrast, we control the light to produce subtle highlights and shadows that will fall well within the latitude of the film. This is the essential lesson for you to learn.

I will suggest ways to experiment with your equipment, but I can't tell you that with a bone implement the main light should be at four feet, an angle of 60°, diffused through two layers of tracing paper, with a twelve-inch piece of poster board to bounce fill. There are too many variables to be considered about the size, shape, depth, texture, and reflective qualities of the artifact, along with any number of possibilities for combining lights and accessories. You will find this entire process much simpler if you begin by understanding how to use the latitude of the film.

EQUIPMENT

The following lists of equipment for the studio may seem endless, but they are offered to suggest suitable alternatives based on need, availability, or budget constraints. Having the patience to do it right is the essential element. Fortunately, your patience is tested less and less as you explore options and gain experience. Start with simple equipment and good technique.

Camera and Lenses

The camera can be the 35mm you have been using for fieldwork. Working with a controlled source of light will achieve better results than will grappling with a large-format studio camera for the first time.

The single lens reflex (SLR) camera, designed to view and meter through the lens, is a good choice. Because the window does not take in the same view as the lens, a rangefinder camera (also notorious for problems with close focusing) is not a good choice. With a reliable through-the-lens (TTL) metering system, you can use any filter without having to calculate a compensating adjustment—saving you the expense of buying a good hand-held meter.

Most SLRs also have the advantage of allowing you to change lenses. A standard 50mm lens is useful for many artifacts, and especially for copying documents. One that incorporates macro (close-up) focusing would also be useful. A zoom lens in the 70mm to 170mm range is an excellent addition because it will reduce the amount of time spent repositioning the camera and tripod. If you don't have a zoom, you'll find that a set-focal-length lens in the 85mm to 105mm range will be a studio workhorse. Again, one that can do macro focusing will be a plus. Longer focal length lenses offer several advantages because they give a more natural perspective of a three-dimensional subject: the angle of view is much narrower (about half that of a 50mm) so that you devote less attention to the backdrop and more to the artifact; you won't have to work so close to the subject that you interfere with lighting; and camera, film, and photographer can be kept out from under the hot lights.

Some autofocus cameras with programmed metering will work well on a tripod if you recognize and respect your minimum focusing distance; the camera will allow you to take a lengthy exposure without a flash; and you are familiar enough with the functions to bracket your exposure, preferably by half stops.

Light Meters

If your camera is one of those excellent quality old-fashioned varieties, it may not have a built-in light meter. A hand-held meter is an essential investment. When shopping for a meter, follow these guidelines:

> *Use the best quality meter you can.* Inexpensive meters are inconsistent meters and a quick route to disappointing results. If your friends all paid less than $300 for their meters, get out there and make new friends.

> *Try to find a good quality used meter.* The best source is usually the small retailer or camera repair shop that you know, one that will be more concerned with reselling only reliable equipment. (Have it checked out thoroughly before buying it.)

> *Consider getting a Gossen Luna Pro.* If you are on an expense account, it's an excellent meter.

Tripod and Cable Release

The sturdier the tripod the better. It takes surprisingly little vibration to blur an image. Even with a tripod, you need to make a point of standing still when taking the picture. Some models come with a horizontal arm in addition to the three legs, which can be convenient in many situations.

Get a long cable release—about 30 inches. Hold it so that it droops with plenty of slack to prevent any jiggles or tugs.

C Clamp

If you need to copy documents occasionally, get a specially designed C clamp. Such a clamp holds the camera on a tripod-like mount, then attaches to a tripod leg so that you can aim the camera down onto a table surface or floor. It will also clamp to a sturdy table or chair leg. A stack of books placed on the table or chair can prevent wobbling.

When the camera is attached to one leg of a tripod, the awkward distribution of weight can cause blurring at the slightest touch. To weight the camera securely in place, hang a bag full of books down through the center of the tripod.

Reversing the head of the tripod to place the camera between its legs is another way you can position the camera straight down. Doing so, however, can make it difficult to get shadowless light on the document. As the center post is extended downward to get the camera closer to the subject, the camera will be prone to a pendulum-type vibration. The camera should therefore be positioned as high as possible when it is between the tripod legs. To get the camera closer to the subject, shorten the tripod legs rather than lowering the center post.

With any of these arrangements for copying, a small level will be useful to make certain that the camera is positioned parallel to your document.

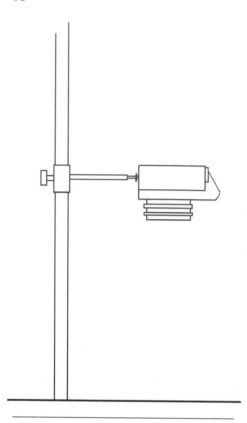

Figure 7.1 Copy stand.

Copy Stand

If you need to copy many documents or illustrations, use a copy stand. This unit consists of a vertical rod attached to a working surface (fig. 7.1). The camera attaches to the rod, is held pointing straight down, and can be raised or lowered to suit the subject. A small level should be used to be sure that the back of the camera is parallel to the document.

Copy stands are made with or without lights attached to them. Because a copy stand can be useful for working with artifacts as well as documents, it may not be to your benefit to pay extra for such stationary lights. Lithics, beads, a small textile, or other relatively flat artifacts may, for example, benefit from a different approach to lighting.

You may get a bargain on a copy stand through a garage sale or newspaper advertisement. Just make sure that the stand is rigid and that the back of your camera is parallel to the base of the stand.

Lights

Tungsten lights are the best choice when getting started in a small studio. The bulbs are readily available, and a functional assembly requires only a small investment ($70 to $100). The brighter light of the large studio alternatives is not necessary when the task is copying documents or photographing small artifacts (see fig. 7.2).

Tungsten DXC and ECT, and the tungsten-halogen DYH bulbs are all commonly available at photo supply stores or at large lighting outlets. You can also purchase the stands and reflectors that go with the ECT bulbs, but some less expensive (and less convenient) choices are available in large hardware stores.

A significant advantage of studio photography is the ability to control light placement. If necessary, you can get by with one light and a simple reflector. At least, after struggling to make do with this arrangement, you will appreciate having two lights more than someone who just went out and bought them to begin with. Using two matched lights is important when the task is copying documents.

The tungsten DXC and ECT bulbs work with common screw-in sockets and are less expensive to replace than the tungsten-halogen DYH. They also have a significant drawback: the DXC and ECT bulbs may burn for a hundred hours, but the output dims rapidly. After only three or four hours, the dimming will affect color balance. This is of no concern if you plan to use black-and-white film either exclusively or in addition to color. When it is time to photograph in color, you can arrange the lights to use older bulbs to view the scene, then switch briefly to fresher ones to take the picture.

Steady dimming also means that lights should be used and replaced in pairs. (Maintaining uniformity is critical when copying documents.) You should plan to buy four tungsten bulbs initially, then maintain this stock with two fresh lights. To have one of your last two bulbs quit halfway through a shooting is, at best, discouraging. If your project demands a fair amount of excellent color reproduction and you will not be using up the balance of the life of these bulbs with black-and-white film, the tungsten-halogen DYH type of bulb will be a better investment. If the bulbs are to be used in a school or museum setting where more than one person will be using the lights, it will

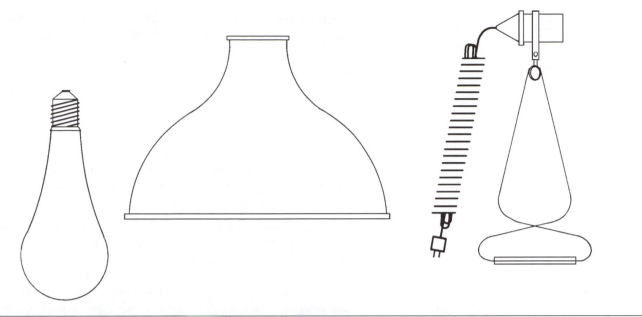

Figure 7.2 Bulb, reflector, socket, and clamp.

be harder to keep track of which ones have been used and for how long.

All bulbs should have a 3200 Kelvin color temperature; 3400 Kelvin bulbs (a light blue) are available but would require a filter if used with common tungsten film.

Built-in Reflectors: Some floodlights such as the 250- to 500-watt DXC have a built-in reflector; so, you do not need to purchase a separate exterior reflector. Bulbs are $10 to $15 each. Make sure that the light has:

Ceramic socket and attached cord. Plastic sockets are more common, but they get too hot for this type of bulb and pose a fire hazard. Cords should be of a heavy-duty variety. Socket and cord cost $8 to $12.

Clamp. This device needs to fit around the socket at one end and to clamp onto most anything to hold it in place. Cost is about $5.

Two supports. The lights are clamped to these supports, which are a bit more functional if they can be moved easily. Stands should tolerate heat and be sturdy enough so that they will not tip over with a bump. You could use a pole or floor lamp, the back of a tall chair or bar stool, PVC pipe and your imagination, a tree stand with a wood "tree" standing four to six feet tall made from a two-by-two piece of wood, or a music stand, a microphone stand, or even a light stand.

ECT Tungsten with Added Reflector: If you already have aluminum reflectors ($5 to $10 each), you can use the less-expensive ECT photo flood bulbs ($8 to $12 each). Double-check the socket to make certain it is ceramic.

Tungsten-Halogen Unit: For several hundred dollars you can get two Acme or Victor lights (or their equivalents). They use the 650-watt DYH quartz halogen bulbs and produce a uniform light (even intensity and even color) over the life of the bulb. They also burn much longer than tungsten bulbs. (If you ever dismissed the importance of turning out lights to save energy, the cost of replacing these bulbs will convert you.) If these lights are within your budget, purchase the type with a built-in holder for glass dichroic filters. These filters will balance the light for use with daylight films, so that you don't have to use this dark blue filter over the camera lens. Removing the filter from the camera makes focusing easier, with no risk of diminishing resolution.

Accessories to Bounce or Diffuse Light

By diffusing the *key light*, you can eliminate burned-out highlights. With a reflector or second light that is less intense, you can use a *fill light* to balance contrast and keep otherwise dark shadows well within the film's latitude.

The type and placement of the accessories used to achieve this balance are limited only by the imagination of the photographer. Bouncing light off a colored surface will adversely influence the color of the photograph. Avoid using a white reflector that has yellowed with age or working next to a wall that has been painted a color other than flat white. Lights can be reflected off such items as:

> *Small studio umbrella.* This umbrella, which may have an opaque silver or white interior, is an efficient way to bounce light with very little loss of intensity. It may be possible to attach it to your light stand or to use it on an independent stand.

> *Foamcore.* This is a rigid board (available through photo supply or art supply stores) with a very white surface that reflects light well. Foamcore is susceptible to yellowing with age. Cut off a small corner of the new board and store the piece in an envelope away from light, so that you can compare the two pieces occasionally to check for discoloration.

> *Posterboard, a flat white wall, or anything else you can paint white or cover with the dull side of a piece of aluminum foil.*

To hold a tabletop reflector in place, use a small vise or several clothespins nailed to a block of wood or stuck in modeling clay.

Lights can be diffused through such items as:

> *Diffusing box.* This box attaches to your light source and is available at photo supply stores. Anything that is attached to a light should be designed to stand up to the intense heat the light generates.

> *Rigid sheet of white acrylic plastic or clear plastic covered with tissue or tracing paper.* Mount it on a stand between the light and the subject, prop it up, clamp it to the edge of a table, or have an assistant hold it. Some plastics manufacturers will have good sized scraps available.

> *Tracing paper, frosted Mylar, or fabric.* Tape or staple these to a frame that has been nailed together or cut from corrugated cardboard.

> *Roll of tracing paper or frosted Mylar.* Rolling it into an eighteen-inch width will probably make it rigid enough to stand on edge and encircle the subject. Lights can be placed outside this circle at varying distances for appropriate highlight and fill intensity. The ends can be left open for the camera, a hole can be cut out of a complete circle, or you can shoot from the top down into this circle.

Working Surfaces

It is an advantage to vary the height of your working surface to suit light placement or an artifact that is best photographed from the top. Collect an assortment of tables or rigid boxes of various heights. If your tripod does not have an extending arm to hold the camera over the subject, a small table that fits between the legs of the tripod will be helpful.

Backgrounds

By definition, a background should never intrude. Therefore, take the effort to eliminate shadows that fall onto the background and cause it to become noticeable. Avoid taking attention away from the subject by backing it with hot pink or a straw placemat. Absolutely nothing should draw attention to the background.

Official background paper is available. A six-foot-wide roll will run about $20. Heavy white paper, such as butcher paper, also works well— as long as it has a dull finish. Heavy weight paper will drape better and is less likely to wrinkle. Black velvet will also do a good job. A minimum workable size of any background would be two to three feet wide and four to six feet long. A 50mm lens will take in more background than a telephoto; so, plan the width accordingly.

White and black are recommended because they cause no random color influence. Black also handles minor shadows very nicely. Placing the backdrop is just a matter of tacking one end to a wall, probably two feet or so above your table, and letting it drape over the table for a seamless, horizonless background (fig. 7.3).

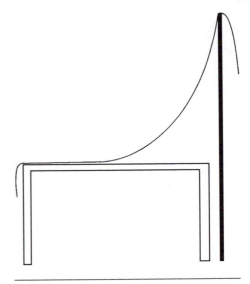

Figure 7.3 Table, drape of background tacked to wall.

Props

Props can hold an artifact or scale in their most revealing position. The most suitable prop is the one that works. Modeling clay, wads of masking tape, a Styrofoam cube, little blocks of wood, beanbags—all are useful. If it is at hand and it works, it is a prop.

Color Bars and Gray Scales

A color bar is made up of various color patches, and a gray scale contains shades of gray from white to black. Kodak makes very nice ones in various sizes and at a reasonable cost. If your photographs are to be published, the engraver and/or separator will want a color bar and gray scale included to reproduce color accurately. Put them at the edge of the picture so that they may be cut out when printed.

FILM AND CORRECTING FILTERS

Of the five groups of film listed below, the first two (tungsten and black-and-white) do not need any color-balancing filters. The others will need corrective filters.

Tungsten Balanced Color Slide

Ektachrome 50 Tungsten Professional

Ektachrome 160 Tungsten

Fujichrome RTP 64 Tungsten

Black-and-White Film

High resolution plus good latitude is suggested for artifacts, for copying a photograph or illustration that includes colored or gray areas, and for retaining all the detail in a handwritten page. All are negative films for prints. (See chapter 3 for suggestions on film for black-and-white slides.)

>   *Agfapan 25*
>
>   *Ilford Pan F 50*
>
>   *Kodak Technical Pan 25* (and low-contrast processing)
>
>   *Kodak T-Max 100*

Below are some high-resolution and high-contrast choices for copying line drawings, a page of type, or charts and graphs. The subject should not contain any gray or mid-tones of color. The first three are black-and-white negative films; they produce a print that duplicates your original. A frame from this strip of negatives can be put into a slide mount to project a reversed white-on-black graphic. The last two are positive (instead of negative) films. When they are mounted and projected, you will have a very sharp black-on-white graphic like your original artwork. (See also appendix D.) Do not risk using any of these touchy films during fieldwork without testing them at home first:

>   *Kodalith 8*
>
>   *Kodak High Contrast Copy 64*
>
>   *Kodak Technical Pan 100* (and high-contrast processing)
>
>   *Kodak Ektagraphic HC 8* (positive)
>
>   *Kodak LPD 4* (positive)

If you want to try a copy film, you'll need to find a lab that will process it (unless you are prepared to develop it yourself). It is made by Kodak, but that does not mean that Kodak will process it. Because of low demand, usually only an independent lab will offer the special handling required.

Find the lab, then buy the film they suggest. Some copy films are recommended for use only with uniform studio lights. Even with these films, it is possible to get good results with a graphic taped to a fence in bright sunlight. It is essential to meter from a gray card and bracket the exposure by half stops.

Reciprocity and ISO

When you load a film with an ISO of 8 or 4, one of the first things you notice is that the camera does not have these ISO settings. Built-in metering systems seldom have an ISO setting lower than 25. Nor do these films have the DX encoding on the canister to set the ISO automatically.

Use all you have learned about reciprocal settings to calculate a good exposure. For example, I figured the reciprocal settings shown below after coming up with a meter reading, at ISO 25, of f/16 for one second. The process is as follows:

1. I know an ISO 12 film is going to require an exposure twice the length of an ISO 25 film. Figuring this two-second exposure at f/16 is the first step.

2. The same doubling of exposure is then calculated for ISO 6 and ISO 3.

3. I then plug in what is referred to as a "darned good guess" to arrive at an estimated exposure for ISO 8 and ISO 4:

ISO	Shutter speed	f-stop
25	1 second	f/16
12	2 seconds	f/16
8	3.5 seconds	f/16
6	4 seconds	f/16
4	6.5 seconds	f/16
3	8 seconds	f/16

If your camera is set for ISO 25 and you get a reading of one second at f/11, all these exposure lengths could be used at f/11. If you wish to use f/16, begin your calculations with: ISO 25 for two seconds at f/16. These extremely slow films need to be bracketed by one-third or half stops. The slightest over- or underexposure will blow the image. When you have gone to all this trouble, plan to take at least five slightly different exposures.

Using Daylight Color Films Indoors

Any color slide or print film that would normally be used outdoors can also be used under tungsten light. You must use an 80A filter with any daylight film to overcome the yellowish cast that tungsten light produces. The gelatin filters available from Kodak are good for the studio, but they are too fragile for fieldwork.

Because gelatin filters are very thin, they will have virtually no effect on resolution. You will need a holder that screws onto the end of the lens. An alternative to buying this studio-only equipment—and possibly duplicating a good filter you may already have—is getting a very good quality ground-glass filter.

The dark blue 80A filter will reduce light by two and one-third stops. If you are using DXC or ECT tungsten bulbs, it will be easier to focus if you have fresh 500-watt bulbs for the highest output of light.

Maximum Resolution Color Slides

If you need to reproduce exceedingly fine detail with a color slide, three films have an edge over the rest:

Ektachrome 50 Tungsten Professional

Kodachrome 25 (with an 80A filter)

Kodachrome 40 Tungsten Professional (with an 82A filter)

Kodachrome 25 and 40 will need a filter for accurate color. Any filter other than gelatin may reduce this critical resolution, making the unfiltered Ektachrome 50 the best choice.

Professional films should be purchased just before use and handled with care. Here are some handling tips:

- Store the film, still in its plastic can, in a refrigerator.

- Let the film warm to room temperature several hours before removing it from the can and loading it in your camera.

- Studio lights can be hot. Be careful not to let your camera, film, and filter cook alongside the lights.

- When the roll has been shot, put it back in the can and back into the refrigerator.

- Have it processed as soon as possible. The latent image on the exposed film will shift with time and heat.

Note: See appendix D for some tips on preparing slides for presentation.

THREE-DIMENSIONAL SUBJECTS

The tips on assessing an artifact for its most revealing angle and getting it set in a workable position (included in the discussion on photographing artifacts in the field) all apply to the studio.

Even though I cannot tell you what the best light placement is for any particular artifact, I can tell you that you should *never* point an undiffused light source directly at a three-dimensional subject. If you have any doubt about why, remember what you have learned about keeping both highlights and shadows within the latitude of the film.

When using just one light, aim it at a piece of foamcore or into an umbrella and bounce this light onto your subject, placing highlights where they best reveal form. Or, you can aim the light at the subject but use a diffuser that is dense enough to reduce intense highlights and mute any sharply defined shadows. Because you can use a lengthy exposure, the artifact does not have to be lit with much intensity. You need just enough light to focus accurately.

When the key light has been positioned to complement the subject, then experiment to find the best angle for the reflector or fill light. Like highlights, shading reveals information about form. The fill light is used to brighten shadows so that they do not obscure information and to retain shading that conveys dimension. If the key light casts a shadow that is not suitably diminished by the fill, move the key light farther away from the subject or use a more dense diffuser. If the fill light or reflector creates a second set of shadows, both lights are too intense.

Taking the time to make minor adjustments is as important as any piece of equipment. When the view through the lens looks perfect:

1. Check the depth-of-field chart (in chapter 1) to discover the f-stop you should be using for the depth of field that the subject needs.

2. Double-check the ISO setting on the camera for the film you are using.

3. If the film needs a balancing filter, put it on the camera before metering.

4. Place the gray card over the subject so that it is in the same light as the artifact and you are looking at it straight on. You have already set the

f-stop; the meter reading will therefore determine the length of the exposure.

5. Attach the cable release to the shutter.

6. Recall that depth of field is one-third in front and two-thirds behind the exact point you focus on. Make the best use of the depth of field by focusing at a point that is behind the front surface of the artifact.

7. If your camera has a mirror lockup, use it to avoid *mirror slap* (see below).

8. Take the picture.

9. Bracket this exposure with a slight overexposure and a slight underexposure.

Your proficiency with setting up lights, assessing contrast between highlights and shadows, and attending to pre-exposure details will increase with practice.

MIRROR SLAP

Mirror slap is the slight internal vibration that occurs when the mirror is lifted as the shutter is released, and most cameras are subject to it. It has nothing to do with the sturdiness of a tripod or copy stand, but it can cause a blurred image as though the camera had been moved.

The degree of vibration will vary with the camera's design and overall condition. It is usually most noticeable at speeds of a 30th, a 15th, or an 8th. (Speeds faster and slower than these seem to handle the vibration much better.)

To find out if your camera is a victim of mirror slap, take a couple of test shots of a detailed subject at minimum focus, one with a half-second exposure, and one at a 15th. Use a tripod and a cable release. When the test shots are projected, any problem will be apparent.

If the 15th of a second exposure is blurred, you will need to allow for this vibration when using shutter speeds of an 8th, a 15th, or a 30th of a second. You might start by affixing a permanent reminder to your tripod and copy stand.

Most older cameras have a lever or button that will lock up the mirror (so that you cannot see through the lens). This should be used just before releasing the shutter. The feature of a mirror lockup (but not the vibration) has been dropped from many newer cameras. On some cameras, using the self-timer will lock up the mirror (again, so that you cannot see through the lens). You may simply use the timer to release the shutter, instead of a cable release, when working with these problem speeds. Otherwise, avoid these speeds, especially in critical close-up situations.

COPYING

Most flat documents or illustrations can be copied easily when attention is given to just a few details. Whether the subject is on a wall, floor, or copy stand, the camera must be centered over the subject. When copying a map, don't forget to recenter when you move in for a close-up of just one corner.

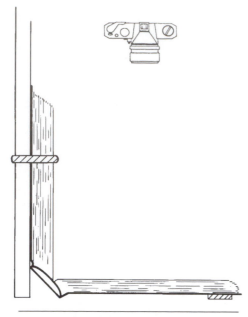

Figure 7.4 Book open 90°.

Use a small level to match the angle of the camera back to the subject. Here's a good procedure to follow:

1. Make sure lights are of uniform intensity.

2. Place the lights at a 45° angle above the subject to reduce reflection or glare.

3. Set the aperture at f/8 for best resolution.

4. Take the meter reading from a gray card to determine the shutter speed.

5. Lock up the camera mirror if possible.

6. Use a cable release to trip the shutter.

7. Bracket the exposure and success will be yours.

Working with a subject that is curled or wrinkled can pose a few problems. If the subject is suitable for photocopying, have it copied onto white cardstock. (This is also a good way to handle a black-and-white illustration from a glossy page.) Rather than laying a piece of glass over the subject to flatten it (which loses resolution), try one of these alternatives:

▪ Take a flat sheet of metal (not aluminum) and spray it flat black. The subject can be placed on this sheet and held down at the edges with magnetic tape. This metal-and-tape frame is flexible, nondestructive, and easy to use.

▪ Use strips of metal, glass, or acrylic to lay over the borders of the original. They must be thin or they will cast shadows.

▪ Place the document on cork and pin at the corners.

▪ Use two-sided tape on the back of the four corners, and a lot of care when removing the tape.

▪ Spray a mat board with a light coat of contact cement and stick your subject to this surface. Any cement that transfers to the back of the subject can be removed with rubber cement pickup. Spray cement and pickup are available at art supply stores. *Do not risk this method with a valuable original.*

▪ Use a vacuum frame. This can be purchased from a printing equipment supply house.

The easiest way to get a page from a book to lie flat is to prop open the book at only a 90° angle (fig. 7.4). Use a bungee cord or a length of elastic to secure the upright half to the copy stand arm or a chair leg. Binder clips are handy to flatten pages to the cover. If the book binding extends down and lifts the inside edge of the page, use a wedge under the outside edge to level it.

To kill any color on the facing page you may need to cover the page with a piece of white poster board. If printing from the back of the page shows through, a piece of black construction paper placed under the page will hide it.

Eliminating Reflections

Even though you have taken pains to make sure that the subject is flat and the lights are at a 45° angle, the photo of a glossy page or a document in a frame may still be ruined by the reflected glare. Getting rid of all other room light may help. However, what you will most often see reflected in the subject is the camera itself.

Take a piece of flat black poster board that is only slightly larger that your subject. Cut a hole in the center of the board to fit it over the camera lens. Then run a piece of masking tape from one end across the back of the camera to the other end to hold the board in place (fig. 7.5). If the ends of the tape still cause a reflection, cover them with a black marker.

Polarizing

Reflections are evident with a shiny subject, but they can also fade color intensity from a dull surface. You may be able to eliminate all glare with a polarizing filter (see chapter 4, "Polarizing Filter").

Have both of the lights and the camera lens positioned in a straight line (on the same plane left to right). To test the polarizer, place a shiny coin, paper clip, or glass from a small picture frame in the center of the subject. See if all bright reflections disappear as the filter is turned. If so, make sure the filter stays in this position through the final focusing and when the meter reading is taken from the gray card.

If glare persists, you will need to polarize the lights as well as the lens. Polarizing screens that are placed between light and subject are available at a well-stocked photo supplier. You will need one for each light; they cost $40 to $50 each. They must be placed a few inches in front of the lights because of heat; so, two more stands or light attachments will be necessary.

Like the filter on the lens, these screens have an axis to work with. When positioning these screens, align both axes identically—both vertical or both horizontal. Now get your paper clip back down there. Rotate the polarizing filter on the camera lens until every last highlight disappears. Retain this filter position while fine tuning the focus, get the meter reading from a gray card, and shoot.

This cross-polarizing technique can also be used to get very rich color out of textiles and painted ceramics. If you need to get an excellent reproduction of a high-gloss subject, textile, or paint, the investment could be worthwhile.

Revealing Texture

When a document contains raised lettering, two uniform lights will cast two shadows. This makes the letters difficult to read; so, we are going to work with only one set of shadows. The key light is first placed where it will cast just enough shadow to best reveal form. Humans expect to see shadow at the bottom of a page and not at the top. In order for a photograph to be read easily, the light should be coming from the top so that the shadows fall beneath the lettering. Place the key light high enough to give uniform coverage to the rest of the document. This also keeps shadows from being lengthened distractingly. All you need is a small shadow for definition.

Once again, the next step is to reduce contrast—the shadow should not be confused with the black of the ink. You can use a reflector or fill light to brighten these shadows, but limit its intensity to avoid casting a second set of shadows. This method of using an intentionally directional light to bring out texture can also be applied to textiles, a reasonably flat artifact that has been incised, worked bone or shell, and many lithics.

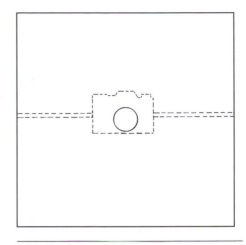

Figure 7.5 Black cardboard used to hide camera reflection.

Chapter Eight

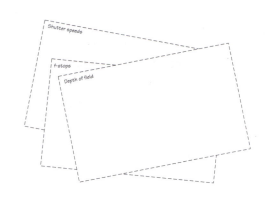

Review

*E*valuating photos from previous fieldwork (or your last vacation) can be the perfect opportunity to reinforce your understanding of basic technique and to make note of problems that need attention. (The troubleshooting guide in appendix A will also help.) Pictures don't turn out for many reasons. Don't give up. You can become proficient with a 35mm camera—with enough practice.

ASSESS YOUR WEAKNESSES

Start by assessing your photos for sharpness, depth of field, and exposure.

Sharpness

Should you be using a faster shutter speed or a tripod? Pay particular attention to any low-light scenes and close-ups. (Your choice of film and camera lens will also influence sharpness.) Assess your skill at hand-holding the camera by taking the same shot at both a slow and a fast speed.

Depth of Field

Is all of the subject sharp? Is the foreground blurred? Does the background distract from the subject? Would it have been better out of focus? Is the camera placed at the best angle for the subject? If you had used a tripod and very small aperture, would the result have been better? Did you miss much because only a part of the picture is sharp?

Exposure

Check out very light and very dark areas. Was important information lost? If so, why? What threw off the metering? Were you expecting the film to record too much? Should you have taken one picture for the light area and one for the dark? Are you getting accurate color when you need to? Do you need a system to remind you to set the correct film speed on your camera? (Try taping down the lid on each can of film—when the tape is removed, check the speed setting.)

Don't expect to remember all this the next time you take a picture. Start by identifying a problem or two. Write each one on an index card with ways to correct it. Then go buy yourself a roll of film and try to put your assessment into practice. (Put your cards in your camera case for a quick review every time you use the camera.) Get in the habit of keeping notes on what you do as you take pictures. For example, write down the frame number, subject, and anything unusual about the way you take the picture. In the field, this information will go in your photo log. The review material in the rest of this chapter has been organized into sample cards so that you can use them as a model when preparing your own. As you use the camera and get more comfortable with it, your skills will improve incrementally. Make a point of coming back to this text for a refresher.

ARTIFACTS

- A photograph of any artifact will be its most revealing if the subject is in a subdued light, a light that limits the intensity of both highlights and shadows.

- Reduce the degree of contrast to work within the latitude of the film, ensuring that details are not lost in areas that are too bright or too dark. Use a gray card.

- When the subject is close, depth of field is minimal. Consider the best angle for the subject and focus carefully to place that small area of sharpness where it is needed most.

- The slightest camera movement is exaggerated and will blur details; so, use a tripod.

- Try to get a large detailed image. Situate the camera and tripod to match the most important plane of the subject and get as close as possible.

STEPS TO A SHARP IMAGE WHEN YOU'RE IN A HURRY

- Try to diffuse light as much as possible by shading the subject. If you must use direct sunlight, try to reduce contrast by reflecting light into dark shadows.

- Include a scale.

- Match the angle of the camera to the most revealing angle of the subject to use whatever depth of field is available.

- Use a gray card. If you do not have a gray card, make certain that metering is not thrown off by a high-contrast background.

- Bracket your exposure to make sure that details in highlights and shadows are recorded.

- Reduce camera shake with deep, steady breathing. Wait to squeeze the shutter until the end of an exhale.

- Get complete notes on the location, owner, provenience, and dimensions.

SHUTTER SPEED

- A slight overall loss of detail can indicate problems with a too-slow shutter speed.

- Avoid using a hand-held shutter speed that is much slower than the focal length of your lens. With a standard 50mm lens, a 60th of a second should be your slowest hand-held speed. With a 135mm lens, the slowest recommended speed is 125th of a second.

- Hold the camera carefully when using the minimum recommended speeds and use a tripod when shooting at slower speeds.

- Use extra caution when taking close-ups. The slightest movement will be exaggerated.

F-STOPS

- Small f-numbers (2, 2.8) indicate a large aperture, which means increased amount of light gathered and reduced depth of field.

- Large f-numbers (22, 16) indicate a small aperture, which means reduced amount of light gathered and increased depth of field.

- Speed and f-stop increments are reciprocal. The combinations below will all produce the same exposure. Without remetering, you can move to a more desirable f-stop or shutter speed: f/11 at 250th, f/16 at 125th, or f/22 at 60th

- If you reduce light by moving to a smaller aperture (from f/11 to f/22), you must add light by going to a longer shutter speed (from a 250th of a second to a 60th).

DEPTH OF FIELD

- The distance, near to far, that is going to be sharp in the final photograph is the depth of field. You can't see this zone of sharpness when you look through the viewfinder.

- The point at which you focus is one third of the way into the depth of field.

- Depth of field changes with variations in the f-stop.

- Depth of field decreases when you change to a lens with a longer focal length, which is also true if, for example, you adjust a zoom lens from 35mm to 80mm.

- Depth of field changes depending on the distance to the subject. Focusing close to a subject, for example, reduces depth of field.

- The plane of the film (the back of the camera) should be matched to the most important plane of the subject.

DEPTH-OF-FIELD GUIDE

- The depth-of-field guide on the lens relates pairs of f-numbers to the distance scale. Each number has a line leading to the distance scale. Depth of field is read *from* the distance scale *in between* these pairs of f-numbers. If the lens is set at f/16, for example, the distance that is read between the pair of 16s will be sharply in focus in the photograph.

FILM SPEED AND LATITUDE

- The speed of a film is indicated by its ISO rating.

- The ISO rate is determined by the film's sensitivity to light. A film that is extremely sensitive to light needs only a small amount of light to record an image and is called a fast film. Because it takes less light to get a good exposure, you can use fast shutter speeds.

- The range of dark to light in which the film can make distinctions is called its *latitude*. The range is narrow, much more limited than what the eye can perceive.

- Latitude varies slightly according to film type. Generally, with color slide film, any part of the scene that is two or more f-stops away from the metered exposure will be so dark or light that most detail will be lost.

USING A GRAY CARD

- A metering aid called a *gray card* is a piece of neutral gray cardboard that reflects a specific amount of light. Its medium is the tone the light meter tries to achieve with its recommended exposure.

- For pictures of artifacts, for copying graphics, or for any scene where the contast will throw off the light meter, meter from a gray card rather than from the subject. When you're setting up a picture, hold this card in front of the subject until you see plain gray through the lens, then set the f-stop and shutter speed.

EMERGENCY GRAY CARD

If you have lost or left your gray card behind you can use:

- A nonreflective brown paper bag or burlap sack—either will come within (about) one f-stop of being a gray card. (Overexpose a reading taken from the bag by one f-stop.)

- The palm of your hand. Again, overexpose the reading by one f-stop. Hold your hand in the same light as the subject and get the camera close enough to make sure that the reading is only from your palm.

- In a dark, dense jungle or forest, a highlighted patch of green foliage. Meter on this brighter tone to get a good neutral exposure.

- On a clear day, in morning or afternoon sun, meter the dark blue sky *away* from the sun. Be sure not to include land or clouds, just dark blue sky.

BRACKETING EXPOSURES

- *Bracketing* is a term used to describe the practice of taking several exposures of the same scene.

- Make a practice of bracketing your exposure. You don't want to lose important data because you set the wrong film speed, failed to recognize a problem with high contrast, or worked with weak batteries that gave incorrect meter readings.

- It is not always possible to guess which part of the subject is best for the meter reading. Bracketing will help you get the shot even if your first choice is wrong. Make sure that the data collection is as complete as possible.

- The significance of a feature may not be obvious at the time a picture is taken. In the field, you are in no position to judge the importance of something in the shadows. So, bracket your exposure.

LIGHT

- Bright sunlight is good for photographing the whole site when its features are most distinct.

- Lightly overcast weather (as well as the minutes just before sunrise or just after sunset) is very good for the features of a grid or profile.

- Heavy overcast weather (or uniform shade) is great for photographing artifacts.

- Be alert to high-contrast scenes.

- Meter the subject (the most important part) of the picture only.

PHOTO LOG

- Record the date, roll number, frame number, essential grid coordinates or artifact catalog number, and a brief description. For example,

  7-27-89 #14 [frame #], PV74-1-325-34 [cat. #], painted rim sherd

- Take a few seconds to jot down other observations because they can fade fast.

- Include the direction you are facing when photographing a site or grid.

- Make a sketch. If the picture is a view of three grids, for instance, show the relationship and identify each.

- Make a note of the time on two or three occasions during the day to help reconstruct sequences.

- Identify any landmarks in a panoramic photo

- Make a note of the height of the wall even if the stadia rod appears perfectly legible.

TAKING THE COMPREHENSIVE VIEW

- Toward the end of your fieldwork, take some time to gather a comprehensive record of the site.

- Make the first picture a single shot of a signboard, noting the site, date, location, and principal investigator.

- Try to see how close you can come to showing the who, what, where, when, and how of the project.

- Be sure to take good notes on the provenience and estimated size of what you photograph. This information is frequently forgotten by the end of a journey.

PROFESSIONALISM

- Make sure catalog numbers and scales are legible.

- Clean up the grid before taking your picture.

- Make sure that there is no extraneous material intruding into the frame of the picture.

- Take the time to clean your equipment after a day's work. Establish a routine and make it a habit—it'll save you much grief and money.

- Don't underrepresent the subject. Get rid of any wasted space surrounding it.

- "Fill the frame" means filling the picture with a large, detailed image.

CARING FOR LENSES

- Check for moisture. Moisture from rain, condensation, or humidity can cause a blurring fungus growth on an interior lens surface and ruin the lens.

- Check with an expert. Have a repair technician do a quick test for accurate shutter speeds and meter function. See chapter 5.

- Keep lenses and filters clean. Routinely check all exterior surfaces. Clean by moistening a lens tissue with an official lens cleaning solution. (Do not use eyeglass cleaner.) Apply to the lens with minimal pressure in a circular motion. Polish with a dry tissue.

- Handle lenses carefully. Lenses can become misaligned from a drop or jolt. Remember that repairing a lens is usually more expensive than replacing it.

HAND-HOLDING THE CAMERA

- Steady your hands through controlled breathing. Repeat a slow inhale/exhale several times. At the end of an exhale, gently squeeze the shutter button. Taking a deep breath and holding it can actually induce shaking.

- When hand-holding the camera, match the shutter speed to the focal length of the lens. Use caution even with these minimum speeds—camera shake is a common problem:

    With a 50mm lens, use a 60th of a second.

    With a 135mm lens, use a 125th of a second.

    With a 200mm lens, use a 250th of a second.

CAMERA SETTINGS

- Close-ups exaggerate the slightest movement of camera or subject. Use the next highest "minimum" speed (125th with a 50mm lens) or, better yet, use a tripod and cable release.

- As a rule, never shoot at your lowest f-stop. The lower f-stops reduce both resolution and depth.

- Most lenses produce their finest resolution set at two or three f-stops above the lowest stop on the lens (usually around f/5.6 or f/8). If depth of field is not a factor, these middle f-stops access the best resolution the lens can muster.

- Higher f-stops add depth of field, but slightly reduce fine resolution.

- Evaluate the subject for its best angle and carefully match this angle to the plane of the film (that is, the back of the camera).

Troubleshooting

If your photographs are not as good as they need to be, try using the following troubleshooting checklist to discover the solution. Remember, however, that problems can stem from multiple causes. Fortunately, these problems are usually solved by a few adjustments rather than by expensive repair or new equipment. If the diagnosis eludes you after considering the possibilities, take your problem photographs to a shop for advice.

PICTURE IS BLURRED SLIGHTLY OVERALL

Shutter speed too slow for hand-holding the camera? See chapter 1.

Tripod not sturdy enough? See chapter 4.

Mirror slap? See chapter 7.

Fast film caused poor resolution? See chapter 3.

Dirty lens or filter? See chapter 5.

Close-up accessories altered lens optics, detracting from resolution? See chapter 4.

Poor quality or damaged lens? See appendix B.

ONLY PART OF THE PICTURE IS IN FOCUS

Depth of field inadequate? See chapter 1.

Lens damaged or misaligned? See appendix B.

ONLY PART OF THE PICTURE IS EXPOSED

Mirror, shutter, or film advance stuck? See chapter 5.

Speed set incorrectly to synchronize with the flash unit? See chapter 6.

EXPOSURE OF PICTURE POOR

Shutter speed or light meter inaccurate? See chapter 5.

Batteries weak? See chapter 5.

ISO speed incorrectly set on the camera? See chapter 3.

High-contrast scene throwing off reading? See chapter 2.

COLOR REPRODUCTION APPEARS UNNATURAL

Light reflected off a colored wall or background? See chapter 2.

Film heat damaged or old ? See chapter 5.

X rays at airport (carry-on bags or suitcases) caused a color shift? See chapter 5.

Off-brands of film producing strange colors? See chapter 3.

Developing or printing mistake by the processor? See chapter 5.

Choosing a New Lens

If you have checked all the possibilities in appendix A and are still unhappy with the resolution of your photographs, you may need a new lens. Evaluate need carefully; you will have to pack it. A camera shop should not balk at letting you try a lens. If they won't let you take it home for a test, take a newspaper along, drop it on their sunny sidewalk, and photograph it close up with their lens. Then try the same shot (same light) with your old lens. The results should tell you if you have found the solution to your problem.

Check consumer publications. Keep in mind exactly what features are important to you. All too often these publications compare apples to oranges before arriving at value.

Check photography magazines for benchmark testing of equipment. Examine the data on function or lines per millimeter of resolution. Beware of comparative comments such as "a sharp lens for its class." Test results may show that the lens is no good.

Get the best lens you can afford. Tamron and Sigma offer a line of superior optics, at reasonable prices, that can be added to most any brand of camera.

If you are thinking of replacing your camera, look at Nikon, Canon, Olympus, Pentax, or Minolta for some of the best optics available. Unless you are paying for a lot of bells and whistles on the camera, cost is a pretty good indicator of lens quality.

The Pentax K1000 and Canon T60 are two reasonably priced choices for the beginning student of 35mm. These reliable, basic cameras are backed by a complete line of accessories. Choose Nikon for better optical quality— and a higher price.

Lenses on automatic cameras are usually of lesser quality. Manufacturers cut corners to accommodate the autofocus function, for cost and weight considerations, and because the average user does not need critical resolution.

Make sure that any lens added to your present system retains "automatic" function (that is, it will close *automatically* to the selected f-stop when you press the shutter). You can take a good picture with a lens that is not automatic or one that has become a "manual" because of the addition of an extension tube that does not integrate with your system. However, it is such a demanding process that you'll seldom use it more than once or twice.

Don't pay extra for a lens with an aperture as large as f/1.4 or even f/1.8. These lenses are specially designed for action photography and photojournalism (requiring fast shutter speeds and the attendant large apertures). The resolution is *not* as good as is available on lenses whose minimum aperture is f/2 or higher.

Among lenses by the same manufacturer, a macro lens is optically superior to a standard lens. A lens with a set focal length is optically superior to a zoom lens. Such differences can be very minimal, and current technology is closing the gap. Weigh any such differences against having to carry several lenses, and consider your own tendency to take the time to change lenses.

If you take only one lens into the field, take a good quality 28-to-50mm macro zoom. Fieldwork often requires coping with a limited choice of vantage points. Being able to change a scene rapidly with a zoom lens can be helpful. Twenty years ago, zoom lenses were considered toys and could not begin to match the resolution of a set-focal-length lens. Not so today. A wide-angle lens (or an eight-foot ladder) is indispensable for a comprehensive photo of a grid. This lens will also let you copy a document down to about a four-by-eight-inch size and get a good close-up of an artifact that stands about five inches tall.

For pictures of small artifacts or for the close-ups that demonstrate use or technology, a macro lens (in the range of 80mm to 105mm) is a valuable tool both in the field and in the studio. It is also expensive and another piece of equipment to pack. If you need to improve on the results you are getting with your 50mm lens and close-up accessories, either this set-focal-length lens or a 70-to-150mm macro zoom lens should do it. Because I normally shoot hundreds of artifacts in the field, this lens is worth its weight to me. It is, however, a specialized piece of equipment. Assess your need carefully before investing.

Shop carefully. Camera salespeople are sometimes trained in used car lots and almost always work on commission with bonuses for pushing the overstock of the week. Visit with more than one. I have had very good luck dealing with the small owner-operated shops. They are more concerned with repeat business and are often better schooled in photography.

Sources of Supplies
and Technical Information

AERIAL ARCHIVES

Many government agencies routinely take aerial photos, usually for soil conservation or land management purposes. These photos are most often of a scale too large for discovery, and the light that best meets the needs of soil conservationists is usually a shadowless variety that may not lend itself to revealing archaeological sites. And, unfortunately, no single agency keeps records of everything that is available. The most comprehensive source is the "Status of Aerial Photography in the U.S." from:

Map Information Office
U.S. Department of the Interior
Geological Survey
Washington, D.C. 20242

Additional sources of photographs by region:

Eastern Laboratory/Aerial Photography
11 Tunnel Road,
Asheville, NC 28805

National Air Photo Library
Department of Energy, Mines, & Resources
Surveys and Mapping Branch
615 Booth Street
Ottawa, Ontario K1A 0E9 CANADA

Also check with the local offices of Agricultural Stabilization and Conservation Service, Soil Conservation Service, Forest Service, Geological Survey, Corps of Engineers, Coast and Geodetic Survey, the Air Force, and NASA. Also try state or county planning, land management, highway, agriculture, or forestry departments, or local independent firms that contract for aerial mapping.

ARCHIVAL RESOURCES

Archival photographic materials are available from:

Light Impressions
439 Monroe Avenue
Rochester, NY 14607-3717

University Products, Inc.
P.O. Box 101
Holyoke, MA 01041

Print-File, Inc.
P.O. Box 607638
Orlando, FL 32860-7638

Clear-File, Inc.
P.O. Box 593433
Orlando, FL 32859-3433

Conservation Resources International, Inc.
8000-H Forbes Place
Springfield, VA 22151-2203

MAIL ORDER

These companies sell equipment, film, and/or storage supplies—often for lower prices than retail outlets. Write for a catalog:

Freestyle
5124 Sunset Blvd.
Los Angeles, CA 90027

Porter's Camera Store
Box 628
Cedar Falls, IA 50613

20th Century Plastics
PO Box 30022
Los Angeles, CA 90030

PHOTOGRAPHIC TECHNIQUE

Eastman Kodak Company publishes an abundance of material that will help with most any project. If a particular reference is not in stock at your photo retailer, it can be ordered directly from Kodak. Start by requesting a copy of the *Kodak Index to Photographic Information* (L-1) from:

Eastman Kodak Company
Department 412L
343 State Street
Rochester, NY 14650-0608

Outdoor Photographer is one of the best popular magazines that teaches basic 35mm technique. *Archaeology* magazine also often includes articles dealing with photography, and it is a good place to see examples of excellent photographs. Published site reports are also useful for examples of good (and bad) camera techniques. Notice camera angles, how light affected the results, how depth of field was used, how close the camera was to the subject, and how the picture tells a story.

Slide Presentations

Professional meetings are often your best opportunity to tell others of your research. Slides are an almost essential aid to a presentation. Remember, however, that:

> A *visual aid* is a slide that adds clear, concise information to elaborate a point of your discussion.

> A *visual distraction* is a confusing subject, a chart that is too intricate, a poor exposure, a background that leads the eye away from the subject, or a scene that is out of focus.

Your listeners will, at best, retain only about 30 percent of what you have to say. Aid them with slides that are easy to understand, even from the back of the room. Most high-resolution slide films will stand up just fine to enlargement.

Aiding your viewer is not just good manners. When the members of an audience must work to decipher a photograph, they will hear little of what you have to say. The train of thought will be lost along with any interest. You are there because you have a point to make, and you have a very limited time in which to make it. It is not often that a viewer will seek you out to find out what you were talking about. By giving attention to the following precepts, you can prevent a visual aid from becoming a liability:

> *Use a good quality projector and screen.* Projector lenses, like camera lenses, vary in quality. There is no way to assess the quality of a slide that is projected onto cardboard, a bed sheet, or a wall. Projector lenses need an occasional cleaning, and dim bulbs can hide details in a dark subject. If the picture is blurred slightly overall, the slide projector may be of poor quality or it may need cleaning.

> *Insist that the lights be dimmed.* Room lighting at professional seminars and in classrooms is frequently less than ideal. If you can't modify the light, select slides for your presentation that are of a medium density. The subject should stand out from the background so that it is easily recognized from the back of the room. Dramatically light or dark slides are difficult to see when diluted by ambient room light. Charts using small type—that can only be read from the first row—should not be used.

Check the alignment of the screen to the projector. Slides may be partially out of focus because the screen has not been set *perpendicular* to the projector. Consider the plane of the projected image and match it to the screen.

Mask over a distracting part of a slide (the edge of a table, for example, or a book binding) with polyester tape. Masking should be used on the front, shiny side of the slide (not the dull emulsion side). Half-inch tape is sufficient, and black or silver will work. The tape is available at some art supply stores or through archive supply companies.

REVERSE IMAGES FOR SLIDES

A popular device to dress up a presentation is to reverse a black-on-white graphic for a slide that shows white text on a colored background. The results can be inconsistent; so, don't photograph your artwork using just this method three days before your presentation.

When you have set up to try this technique, also photograph your work with a more predictable film. Use a gray card for metering and bracket everything by half stops. Depending on the intensity of the light, you may be able to hand-hold the camera with Ektachrome; use a tripod with Vericolor. The tone of the background will depend on the exposure and the shade of the filter you use:

Photograph artwork using Ektachrome 100 and a dark yellow filter. You must request C-41 processing instead of the usual E-6 processing. This will give you white lettering on a blue background. The resolution will be good, but not as good as with Vericolor.

Practice with Kodak's Vericolor (ISO 8) for best results. It can produce an extremely sharp slide. The data sheet that comes with it explains all the filter/background color possibilities. Even though Kodak recommends their gelatin filters, a good quality ground-glass filter (yellow, red, or blue) can be used.

Plan to have all artwork ready to shoot. The film should be kept refrigerated (warm to room temperature before loading it into the camera), then processed immediately after use. The first time you try a film like this, bracket extensively (take five or six slightly different exposures). You must use a gray card. See "Reciprocity and ISO" in chapter 7 for calculating reciprocal settings, or use a good hand-held light meter. Keep notes on what you did and what worked the best.

Note: See chapter 7 for black-and-white film choices.

Glossary

aperture	opening in a photographic lens that admits light
ASMP	American Society of Magazine Photographers
ASA number	American standard rating of speed of film (interchangeable with ISO number)
bellows system	system of mounting that extends the lens in which the lens panel and film (focusing) panel move along a central rail, with the two panels connected by a bellows
bipod	a two-legged support
bracketing	technique of photographing a subject at several different exposure settings to ensure at least one exposure will be acceptable or to achieve expressive variations in color saturation, highlights, or shadow details
cable release	camera accessory used for releasing the shutter without touching the camera itself
contact print	a positive image that is the same size as the negative image; made by positioning the negative directly against the printing paper rather than by projecting the image as is done in enlarging
copy film	narrow-latitude film that produces a very high-resolution/high-contrast positive or negative
depth	direct linear measurement from the point of viewing, usually from front to back
depth of field	range in front of and behind a sharply focused subject in which details will also look sharp in the final image

depth of focus	distance through which the film plane can be moved, backward and forward, while retaining the image of an object or point in sharp focus
diffuser	a screen (as of cloth or frosted glass) for softening lighting
diopter	see plus diopter
dichroic filter	filter that affects light by reflecting some wavelengths and transmitting others in contrast to conventional filters that absorb the wavelengths they do not transmit
exposure	total amount of light or other radiant energy received per unit area on the sensitized material, usually expressed for cameras in terms of the time and the lens f-number
exposure meter	a device for indicating correct photographic exposure under varying conditions of illumination
extension tube	ring that fits between the lens and camera, extending the lens and magnifying the image
f-number, f-stop	ratio between the lens focal length and the effective diameter of a given aperture; each setting changes the amount of light passing through the lens by a factor of 2: the light is either doubled or reduced to one-half
field	area visible through the lens of an optical instrument
film speed	sensitivity of photographic film to light expressed numerically as ISO (or ASA) number
focal length	distance of focus from the surface of a lens or concave mirror; distance from the optical center of the lens to the film
Fresnel screen	a focusing screen in which the view becomes sharp when the subject is in focus
gray card	a piece of gray cardboard specifically manufactured for the photographer to aid in determining exposure, lighting ratios, and color balance
high contrast	high degree of difference between the lightest and darkest parts of a picture

internegative	intermediate negative made from a positive transparency or print (or by reversal from an original negative) for use in printing copies
ISO number	international standard rating of speed of film
latitude	range of exposures within which a film or photo will produce a negative or positive of satisfactory quality
lens hood	sunshade that screws onto the end of the lens
macro lens	lens that can focus close and provide high-quality resolution and edge-to-edge sharpness not obtainable using a standard lens; designed for close-up work
mirror slap	slight internal vibration in a camera that occurs when the mirror is lifted as the shutter is released
overexposure	any exposure greater than necessary for optimum image quality
perspective	appearance to the eye of objects in respect to their relative distance and positions
perspective control (PC) lens	a lens that allows limited degree of displacement of image; also called a "shift" lens
plus (+) diopter	diopter: lens whose refractive power is equal to the reciprocal of the focal length in meters; plus diopter: two-element supplementary lens
polarizing filter	filter that causes light waves to vibrate in a definite pattern
pushing a film	using a film at a speed faster than the given ISO speed
rangefinder	device that measures camera-to-subject distance for accurate focusing
reciprocity	range of light intensity x time settings that give equal amounts of exposure (that is, f/8 at 125th of a second, f/11 at 60th of a second, f/5.6 at 125th of a second)
reflex camera	single- or double-lens camera in which the image formed by the focusing lens is reflected onto a screen (usually ground glass) for viewing

resolution	process or capability of making distinguishable the individual parts of an object, closely adjacent optical images, or sources of light
reverse processing	producing a positive rather than a negative
reversing ring	adapter ring that allows mounting 50mm or wide-angle lens inside-out
ring light	flash unit that fits around the end of a lens for close-up subject
shimmering view	see Fresnel screen
shutter speed	speed of operation of a mechanical device that exposes film by opening and closing an aperture (in fractions of a second)
single lens reflex (SLR)	a camera that uses a mirror to bounce the image captured by the lens to the viewfinder
supplementary lens	extra lens element designed to be screwed into the front of a standard lens; element acts by reducing focal length, enabling greater magnification to be achieved for the same lens-to-film distance
soft box	attachment that fits over a strobe so that light is filtered through white fabric
spot meter	type of light meter that can be used up close to meter small areas
split-image screen	a focusing screen in which the two parts of the scene come together for focusing
stability	resistance to chemical change or to physical disintegration
strobe	device that utilizes a flashtube for high-speed illumination in photography
teleconverter	goes between the lens and camera, extending the lens and magnifying the image; has plus diopter built in
TTL	"through the lens"—expression meaning that the camera rather than a flash unit meters the light and controls exposure (in flash exposure)
tungsten film	film that is effective under incandescent, but not fluorescent, light
underexposure	exposure that fails to register tones or details with sufficient density to print or be visible with the desired strength
UV	ultraviolet

Bibliography

AERIAL PHOTOGRAPHY AND INTERPRETATION

Banta, M., and C. M. Hinsley
  1986 *From Site to Sight: Anthropology, Photography, and the Powers of Imagery.* Cambridge, MA: Harvard U Press.

Davidson, Thomas E., and Richard Hughes
  1986 Aerial photography and the search for Chicone Indian town. *Archaeology,* 39(4):58-76.

Eastman Kodak Company
  1985 *Photography from Light Planes and Helicopters* (M-5). Rochester, New York: Eastman Kodak.

Harp, Elmer, editor
  1975 *Photography in Archaeological Research.* Albuquerque: U of New Mexico Press.

Riley, D.N.
  1987 *Air Photography and Archaeology.* Philadelphia: U of Pennsylvania Press.

St. Joseph, J.K.S., editor
  1966 *The Uses of Air Photography.* New York: John Day Co.

Vogt, E.Z., editor
  1974 *Aerial Photography in Anthropological Field Research.* Cambridge, MA: Harvard U Press.

Wilson, D. R.
  1982 *Air Photography Interpretation for Archaeologists.* New York: St. Martin's Press.

Wilson, D.R., editor
  1975 *Aerial Reconnaissance for Archaeology.* London: The Council for British Archaeology, Research Report no. 12.

ARTIFACTS

Callahan, E.
  1987 Metallic powder as an aid to stone tool photography. *American Antiquity* 52:768-772.

Simmons, H.C.
  1969 *Archaeological Photography.* New York: University Press.
    Simmons uses large-format cameras but offers good examples of photographing artifacts in situ and using lights in the studio.

CLOSE-UP TECHNIQUE

Lefkowitz, L.
  1979 *The Manual of Close-up Photography.* American Garden City, New York: Photographic Book Publishing Co., Inc.

Shaw, J.
  1987   *Closeups in Nature.* New York: AMPHOTO.

EXCAVATIONS

Conlon, Vera M.
  1973   *Camera Techniques in Archaeology.* New York: St. Martin's Press.
         *Though Conlon does not work with 35mm, the book contains useful examples
         of site photography.*

Dorrell, Peter
  1989   *Photography in Archaeology and Conservation.* Cambridge U Press.
         *Dorrell includes some good examples of site and artifact photography, and
         elaborate strategies for conservation. Field techniques are complex and
         suited to the advanced photographer.*

Harp, E., editor
  1975   *Photography in Archaeological Research.* Albuquerque: U of New Mexico
         Press.
         *Some good discussion of objectives, but suggestions for meeting various goals
         are often beyond the means of a small project.*

Levine, Aaron M.
  1986   Excavation photography—A day on a dig. *Archaeology* 39(1):34-39.
         *Levine uses more assistants than will be found on most projects, but he offers
         practical advice for photographing an excavation with a 35mm camera.*

Simmons, Harold C.
  1969   *Archaeological Photography.* New York: University Press.
         *This book contains good advice on profiles, using filters, and working with
         artifacts. The suggestions on cameras and accessories are obsolete or
         impractical.*

EXTREME CLIMATES

Eastman Kodak Company
  1988   *Photography Under Arctic Conditions* (C-9). Rochester, New York: Eastman
         Kodak.
  1987   *Tropical Photography* (AC-24). Rochester, New York: Eastman Kodak.

Time-Life Books
  1981   *Special Problems,* Life Library of Photography. Alexandria, Virginia: Time-
         Life Books.

FILM

American Society of Magazine Photographers (ASMP)
  1984   *Stock Photography Handbook.* New York: American Society of Magazine
         Photographers, Inc.
         Contains information on archival quality film.

PHOTOMICROGRAPHS

Eastman Kodak Company
  1988   *Photography Through the Microscope* (M-5). Rochester, New York: Eastman
         Kodak.

STUDIO TECHNIQUE

Eastman Kodak Company
  1985   *Set Up Your Home Studio.* Volume in The Kodak Library of Creative
         Photography, Eastman Kodak & Time-Life Books.
         *Includes excellent examples of studio light placement, diffusion, backlighting,
         and backgrounds, many of which employ everyday materials such as card-
         board and tracing paper.*

UNDERWATER PHOTOGRAPHY

Werner, Steve
  1990   Light in the sea. *Outdoor Photographer* 9(6):34-88.

Index

LIBRARY
ST. LOUIS COMMUNITY COLLEGE
AT FLORISSANT VALLEY

Archaeological Research Tools
from The UCLA Institute of Archaeology

The Student's Guide to Archaeological Illustrating, Revised Edition

Edited by Brian D. Dillon

For the archaeologist with no formal training in art or drafting, this guide covers such topics as basic tools and techniques, rendering of maps, architectural floor plans and reconstructions, stratigraphic sections, relief monuments, ceramics and figurines, burials, artifacts of shell, bone, and lithics, and illustrating from photographs.

1985 185 pages 0-917956-38-9

Practical Archaeology, Revised Edition

Edited by Brian D. Dillon

Papers on chemical reduction of clay matrices, methods of establishing precise provenience, surface collecting using transits, simplified mapping techniques, and use of X rays in artifact analysis.

1989 141 pages 0-917956-64-8

A Conservation Manual for the Field Archaeologist, Second Edition

Catherine Sease

Manual of conservation techniques, oriented to problems archaeologists face in the field. Information on methods and materials, correct handling, packing, and storage techniques, safety procedures, molding and impression techniques, and chemical solution preparation.

1992 192 pages 0-917956-77-X

Scientific Analysis in Archaeology

Edited by Julian Henderson

Presenting a wide range of practical examples using scientific analysis applied to archaeological materials, this book places its emphasis on interpretation of results rather than on techniques. (Co-published with Oxford University Committee for Archaeology.)

1989 313 pages 0-917956-66-4

An Archaeologist's Guide to Chert and Flint

Barbara E. Luedtke

A comprehensive guide to chert analysis, including chapters on its nature, its origins, chemical, visual, and mechanical properties, and possible sources of variation.

1992 172 pages 0-917956-75-3

For more information or to order a title, write to:

UCLA Institute of Archaeology Publications
405 Hilgard Avenue
Los Angeles, CA 90024-1510